DATE DUE			

Eclipse of an Aristocracy

An investigation of the ruling elites of the city of Córdoba

JUAN CARLOS AGULLA

English translation by
Betty Crouse

The University of Alabama Press
University, Alabama

Contents

Preface

This volume presents the results obtained from an empirical investigation, sociological in nature, as to the function that the so-called aristocracy has fulfilled in the power structure of the city of Córdoba; in effect, it studies the power structure of a community. This work is the continuation of an already published series of studies carried out on the same theme. When concluded, all of them together should form a more or less complete study on the power structure of an urban community which, for various reasons, presents characteristics more or less significant for understanding the process of development of a community.

Many people have knowingly or unknowingly collaborated in the collection and interpretation of data. Among these individuals one must mention especially the members of the Cordobese aristocracy who acted as key informants; their information, ideas, experiences, and advice have been of inestimable value in the material realization of this investigation. I do not believe it would be appropriate to single out these individuals, but I wish to thank them for their continuing help and express my most profound appreciation, which even though in simple terms is no less sincere.

This investigation was carried out under the sponsorship of the *Centro Argentino por la Libertad de la Cultura*, which is the Argentine branch of the *Instituto Latino Americano de Relaciones Internacionales (I.L.A.R.I.)* with headquarters in Paris. I would particularly like to thank Mr. Horacio D. Rodríguez, Permanent Secretary of the Center, for his confidence and for the patience with which he accepted my excuses for delaying this publication. Collection of data was done with the collaboration of the Misses Yolanda Gil Fiorenza, Victoria Galvani, Ana María Brígido, Ana Geralnik, and Mrs. Nidia C. de Molina; Mrs. Beba A. de Gaitán was secretary and had a difficult and laborious task of organization; I remain deeply grateful to all these ladies.

This acknowledgment would not be complete if one did not mention the advice and evaluations rendered, during various periods of the investigation, by my colleagues and friends Enrique Luis Revol, Fernando Martínez Paz, and Ernesto Garzón Valdés, whose knowledge of the situation studied has been of great usefulness to me; their patient and sustained dialogue in long informal conversations will perhaps be discovered in many pages of this work. Finally, I would like to express appreciation for the friendship of Professor Delbert C. Miller with whom, together with Dr. Eva Chamorro Greca, I began the first studies on the power structure. To all these persons I would like, expressly, to dedicate this modest book.

Córdoba, December 1967   Juan Carlos Agulla

Power Structure and Social Stratification

ONE In earlier sociological investigation on the power structure of the city of Córdoba, it was manifest that the power structure of an urban community which is found in a certain stage in the process of industrial development has two basic characteristics: on the one hand, a conflicting and inconsistent structural composition, owing to the contiguous and super-imposed presence of elements belonging as much to a residual as to an emerging form of power and, on the other hand, a tendency of the power structure to integrate itself into a definite form—thus functionally surmounting its structural conflict and inconsistency—through the action of a process of industrial development which, in order to succeed, must continue progressively and steadily.[1] To a great extent, this composition and this integrating tendency defined the power structure of a community which is found in a certain stage in the process of industrial development.

Apparently two variables tended to define the stage of the process of development in which the power structure of Córdoba was found which certainly did not appear in cities of other countries (Seattle and Atlanta in the United States, and Bristol in England) which are found to be another level of development and in which similar sociological investigations were carried out.[2] These (independent) variables were: 1) the incipient state of the industrial development process owing—certainly, among other reasons—to the (relative) recency of

2

its introduction (approximately in the 1950s),[3] and 2) the insertion of this process of industrial development of an urban community into the structural framework of a transitional or developing society.[4]

The conflicts and inconsistencies among the components of the power structure of Córdoba were revealed: 1) in the belonging to distinct social strata by the so-called *top influentials* and *key influentials* of the community; 2) in the representation of conflicting interests of the different institutionalized sectors which participated in decisons taken in the community, and 3) in the exercise of a power parallel between the institutionalized power structure and the power complex made up of groups (formal or informal) which in some way influenced getting something done in the community.[5]

In spite of its incipient state, the industrial development process emphasized more and more these structural conflicts and inconsistencies since some individuals, sectors, or groups tended to encourage them and others to resist them; those who tended towards encouragement appeared as individuals, sectors, or groups emerging from this same industrialization process, while those tending to resist appeared as residuals of the process and, therefore, as those who would be inexorably left behind. Thus seen, the elements of the power structure defined not only the type of structure but also, essentially, a trend of the process of change in the power structure.[6]

TWO Among the residual sectors was found the so-called society and wealth; that is, a part of the community which tended to resist the industrial development process and, when this process seemed empirically inevitable, tended to lose influence in decisions taken in the community. This sector was represented by the traditional families of Córdoba who by virtue of certain criteria (family tradition, name, lifestyle, social prestige, etc.) could make their influence felt to see that something was done in the community,[7] since it was to be assumed that in the past, given the criteria which defined it as a social stratum (an aristocracy), it must have had a great influence in city decisions.

This sector, nonetheless, in spite of losing influence as a social stratum, that is, as a functional part of a social stratification system[8] and, therefore, tending to appear as residual, made itself visible through certain of its members who, on the one hand, appeared among the top influentials and key influentials of the community, and on the other appeared as representing other sectors which were emerging from this same process of industrial development. This duality of participation in the power structure of Córdoba by persons who *belong* to a social stratum (the aristocracy) and who *represent* institutional sectors which emerge from a process of industrial development ought to be more fully analyzed as to how a difference between belonging to a social stratum and representing interests of sectors not of this stratum became established.

Ever since the statements of Marx on the social classes and power, theorists on the elites (notably Vilfredo Pareto and Gaetano Mosca) have been struggling with this problem without, as yet, reaching a completely satisfactory solution, trying to explain the relation between power structure and social stratification.[9] At present we are certainly not going to delve into these theoretical statements and even less draw ideological conclusions from the positions which have been adopted.[10] Nevertheless, the investigation carried out in Córdoba touched upon this dilemma in one way or another: whereas, in a moment of time, belonging to a social stratum (in our case, the *Cordobese aristocracy*) was identified with control of the entire power structure, its ruling elites constituting an authentic power elite;[11] yet also, at another point in time, belonging to a social stratum was not identified with total power control; all to the contrary, the ruling elites represented different social strata, did not exercise power in a more or less standard fashion, and represented sectors which

4

to a great extent were conflicting among themselves. It appeared, precisely, that the very process of industrial development was what defined this conflicting situation since it acted as an independent variable of the process of structural change referring to power.

These facts led us to establish some conceptual differences between *power elites,* exercising control (political, economic, cultural, etc.) of the entire power structure, and who exercised this power in a normal fashion (that is, by representing a social stratum), and *ruling elites* who, though representing different institutional sectors of the community in the power structure, did not exercise power in a standard fashion, that is, as belonging to a single social stratum (the aristocracy or the bourgeois, for example), nor could they control the entire community power structure. These conceptual distinctions, by clarifying the theoretical and empirical picture of the Cordoban power structure, facilitated our investigation and, above all, the interpretation of the data gathered.

From these conceptual distinctions arose three working hypotheses that formed the basis of the entire empirical investigation: 1) Córdoba had possessed, at an indefinite moment in time, a *power elite* represented by the *ruling elites* of the different institutional sectors of the community (political, economic, cultural, etc.), who exercised power in a more or less normal manner through being from the same social stratum (the aristocracy) and who controlled the entire power structure, but only when the community was not affected by the process of industrial development. 2) At the time of investigation (since 1963) Córdoba, although it had a power structure (and it cannot be otherwise), did not rely on a *power elite* since the *ruling elites* of the different institutional sectors of the community did not exercise power in a normal way—that is, by representing a social stratum (be it aristocracy, bourgeois, etc.)—nor did they control all the power; but rather its different elements appeared in a conflicting and incoherent form from the structural point of view. 3) The contiguous and superimposed presence in the power structure of Córdoba of *ruling elites* representing strata and institutional sectors of the community which gained as much influence as they lost in decisions taken in the city showed, on the one hand, that the power structure was not controlled by a social stratum and, on the other, that the power structure would tend—in the future, and for as long as the process of industrial development remained constant and progressive—toward the emergence of a new *power elite* formed from the *ruling elites* that would control all the power and do so in a standard manner, by representing a "new" upper class (the bourgeois).[12]

These working hypotheses insinuated the presence of different types of ruling elites, not so much through the institutional sector they represented, as by the function they discharged in the process of community development. In the first place, it was necessary to distinguish between ruling elites representing sectors or strata which lost influence in decisions taken in the community, and ruling élites representing sectors or strata which gained influence in decisions taken in the community. In this work we refer to the first as residual ruling elites and to the second as emerging ruling elites. These designations allowed us to perceive the tendency of the change in the community power structure.

The facts, nonetheless, plainly showed us that there were ruling elites which, although their members belonged to residual social strata (members of the aristocracy), represented emerging institutional sectors (the "industrial or industrialized" sectors). These facts appeared as basic throughout the historical process, since it showed the "hinge" upon which the elites circulated.[13] Consequently, there were residual ruling elites which we designated *traditional ruling elites* and *available ruling elites* with respect to their participation in the community power structure,[14] who exhibited the duality between social stratification and power structure and the tendency of the change in the power structure. The causes which differentiated the residual ruling elites into *traditional* and *available* explained the structural mechanism of the circulation of the ruling elites who relied on this same process of industrial development of Córdoba. We believe that the psychological elements which motivated the "circulation of the elites" to which Pareto referred, with its residuals and derivations, stem from structural causes as was inferred in part by Gaetano Mosca,[15] and not from individual qualities of the elites through belonging to some social stratum (in our case, as members of the Cordobese aristocracy).

If we define the process of change in the power structure of Córdoba—according to the data obtained—as signifying participation in the power structure and in community decisions by the residual ruling elites, be they traditional or available, one can infer that the process of change in the power structure is determined by the manner in which *an aristocracy goes into eclipse,* since the traditional ruling elites move to the fringes of the power structure and the available ruling elites incorporate themselves into the power structure (or continue in it) by representing not their social stratum, but institutional sectors which are forming a "new," still incipient, social stratum (the "new" industrial and financial bourgeois). The fact that one can find, contiguous and superimposed in a given moment of time, different social strata in the power structure because ruling elites belong to them, only points up the transitional stage in which the structure of social stratification is found, since in the uppermost part of the pyramid are found as many social strata belonging to a declining social ordering (the aristocracy, as upper level of an estate system) as those of a system on the rise (the bourgeois, as the high level of a class system); and since, in the passage from a pre-industrial stratification system to a system of industrial stratification, the independent variable defining the change is, exactly, the process of industrial development.[16]

THREE This work proposes precisely to trace, in a fixed period of time, the process of change of the power structure of Córdoba through the gradual and steady eclipse of its aristocracy caused by loss of functions of its ruling elites in the power structure, be they traditional or available. It was presumed that at a certain stage these ruling elites had controlled all the power of Córdoba and had exercised it in a normal fashion, as representing a particular social stratum, the aristocracy; therefore, at a particular time, Córdoba had possessed a power elite. As such, that power elite had, essentially, the function of government. This function of government had to condition the internal structure of the social stratum symbolizing it: the aristocracy.

If the basic hypothesis of the investigation was that the aristocracy went into eclipse while exercising power, that is, in exercising power or functioning as government, it was supposed that the structure of the Cordobese aristocracy also had to undergo changes since its ruling elites ceased being a power elite. And it is precisely this process of loss of influence in the decisions taken in the community to which we refer as eclipse. We are perfectly aware of the limitations involved in explaining the change of the power structure of an urban community through the loss of governing functions of the ruling elites of the Cordobese aristocracy, since it can be much more implicative—and, perhaps, more definitive—to explain it by the increase in governing functions of the ruling elites of the new sectors and social strata emerging from the industrialization process; that is, through the formation of the new social class emerging from this process, the *new bourgeois*. It was our intention at first to make a parallel study of both processes, that is, the eclipse of the aristocracy and the rise of the bourgeois. Lack of time, however, prevented us from carrying out this project. Even though there is already much information and useful material on the formation and growth of the incipient Cordobese bourgeois, as a social strata, we have, with much regret, postponed this study for what we hope is the not too distant future. We have here concentrated on the study of the ruling elites (but not all) of the Cordobese aristocracy. The material at hand on the new Cordobese bourgeois has certainly been of great help in interpreting or evaluating much of the information obtained on the aristocracy. Perhaps the book *De la industria al poder* can in part mend the deficiencies of the present work in that respect.

Prima facie, the data obtained showed that persons belonging to the Cordobese aristocracy tended to figure as ruling elites in the power structure, although they did not represent that social stratum. This fact coùld only be understood by accepting that the ruling elites of the aristocracy, one way or another, were adjusting to the functional demands of the power structure affected by the process of industrial development. This hypothesis, in turn, tended to explain the presence of the ruling elites of the Cordobese aristocracy in the power structure and, above all, to explain the internal changes in the structure of the Cordobese aristocracy, as a social stratum, by the incorporation of new members originating in other social strata. The presence in the power structure of those ruling elites belonging to the Cordobese aristocracy logically led to repercussions in the structure of that social stratum; yet that aristocracy had to possess special characteristics which would permit the "porosity" without losing its character as a social stratum. Therefore arose the necessity of distinguishing between the traditional ruling elites and the available ruling elites.

Confronted with the impact of the process of industrial development of Córdoba, the aristocracy, as a functional social stratum in a system of social stratification, tends to go into eclipse because one part of its ruling elites becomes traditional and, therefore, marginal in the power structure, and the other part of its ruling elites becomes available and, therefore, incorporates (or continues) in the power structure but as a part of (or representing) new social strata (the incipient bourgeois) which, by dint of being new, need the representation (social prestige) of that aristocracy. The traditional sectors of the aristocracy, in the new social stratification system, tend to come down in the social scale, especially as regards power, and their place is taken, exactly, by the emerging sectors of the process of industrial development; the available portion of the aristocracy, in the new social stratification system, retains its place on the social scale, but as a new social stratum, since the criteria for belonging to that social layer have changed and consequently tend to admit new members from other social strata who vary or change the internal structure (that is, the criteria for belonging to the aristocracy) of this same aristocracy. Therefore, a study on the nature and functions which the Cordobese aristocracy fulfilled and fulfills (and perhaps will fulfill) in the power structure is simply the analysis of its eclipse as a social stratum, since the process of industrial development has affected the social stratification because it has changed (or is changing) the ruling elites who control the power. The ruling elites, since they control the power, define the system of social stratification and the position of the different strata within the system; and if these ruling elites do not represent a single social stratum, that is, are not a power elite, the social stratification of the community has, contiguous and superimposed, two systems of social stratification: one which appears as residual and the other which appears as emerging. The process of industrial development will force these ruling elites to homogenize, that is, to represent a new social stratum tied to that process; and thus, the old social strata tend to eclipse from the power structure as they resist this process. Responsibility for the form acquired by the power structure and for the system of social stratification falls on the structure and functions of the ruling elites; therefore, the circulation of the ruling elites determines the mechanisms of social change of a community.[17]

       FOUR The political history of Córdoba of the last few years—in this aspect very closely tied to the political history of the country—presented to us the framework for the investigation we proposed to carry out. The political history of the nation in the last fifty years—as is well known—has been marked by five political incidents which one way or another have influenced the power structure of Córdoba, to the extent whereby the ruling elites (political) were "renewed." These incidents were: 1) the appearance of radicalism in power and, especially in Córdoba, the university reform of 1918; 2) the revolution of 1930; 3) the revolution of 1943; 4) the revolution of 1955, and 5) the revolution of 1966. We do not intend to evaluate these revolutionary happenings; we wish only to establish them as orderly guideposts of empirical data in a study which encompasses almost fifty years of politcal history of Córdoba (from 1916/18 to 1966).

    These revolutionary events have revealed a renewal of ruling elites in the power structure of Córdoba, one could say "all at once"; but also, to a large measure, they marked stages in the development of the power structures of the city.[18] Therefore—irrespective of what they may have achieved or no—these events signified attempts to fit political to social realities, that is, to a process of development of the country in all its manifestations.[19] And this has a certain significance in the changes that the power structure of an urban community undergoes, as it defines four stages or historical periods of Córdoba. In each of these stages we will introduce the ruling elites of the Cordobese aristocracy in order to look at their composition and functions in the community power structure. Consequently, we have four areas or periods of history which, perhaps, correspond to other such circumscribed periods.

In effect, we have a first stage or historical period encompassing 1918 to 1930; a second from 1932 to 1943; a third, from 1946 to 1955, and a fourth from 1958 to 1966. For reasons which are easy to imagine, we have excluded the "revolutionary time" from each period, although at the end of this volume we give these "times" certain special considerations because of the importance they have in the power structure of Córdoba. Within each period we concentrate our study on the ruling elites of the Cordobese aristocracy only, in a "key year" selected on the basis of situations actually very characteristic of the politics of Córdoba (for example, the Federal interventions) which prevented the "neutral" utilization of the middle point since it would represent the zenith of a progressive curve which begins in one revolution and ends in another. Insofar as it was possible—and after a detailed study of the political history of the city—we placed the key year close to this middle and neutral point. In the present study the following key years were chosen: 1924, 1937, 1951 and 1960. As our objective is to trace the trend of the exercise of the functions of government by the ruling elites of the Cordobese aristocracy in the community power structure, we believe the key years are sufficient for showing this clearly. This is the area within which we will move in this volume. The methodology used in the empirical investigation, as well as a table with the most significant historical-political facts of the City of Córdoba between 1918 and 1966, appear in the appendixes of this study.

A Doctoral Aristocracy

ONE If all process of social change means the passing from one structural form to another, and if our objective here is to trace the process of transformation of the power structure of Córdoba between 1918 and 1966, we must clearly have a certain picture (definition) of the power structure before 1918. Only in this way can it be learned by which means and to what extent the object of our study, the Córdobese aristocracy, has changed, since social change is the result of a process of transformation. In the end, then, it is a question of defining the object of our study.

Our definition of the Cordobese aristocracy is the following: the social stratum represented by those who held the power in Córdoba at the beginning of the 20th century. These were the ruling elites, who exercised their power in a normal fashion, that is, by representing a social stratum and, in turn, who controlled the entire power structure; according to what we discovered, it concerned a power elite which exercised power by virtue of its superiority over the common people and in a universally respected form. The characteristics of the ruling elites at the beginning of the 20th century were the same as those of their social stratum: the aristocracy. It was a social stratum which possessed the function of "government" inasmuch as all the ruling elites came from this social stratum.

The reasons for this singular power control by the

Cordobese aristocracy, besides its evident "superiority over the common people" (as stated in contemporary documents) and the respect of the entire population for that fact, can be found in the lack of institutionalized mechanisms which permit a renewal of the ruling elites. Perhaps the ratification of the Sáenz Peña Law created the first institutionalized mechanism permitting this renewal in the components of the Cordobese power structure. If this is true, then logically from that moment on a new situation must be created which arranges the power components in another manner. This process of adjusting to the new situation will be developed in the ensuing chapters. Nevertheless, the consequences of the creation of this mechanism afforded by means of the Sáenz Peña Law were made clear in Córdoba with the university reform of 1918. Therefore, our investigation begins in 1918.

The university reform in Córdoba was something more than a student movement to achieve some reforms in the organization and structure of the old Casa de Trejo. On one hand, it was a social protest movement against the power monopoly of an elite not only academic but also social (the oligarchy) and, on the other, it was the first triumph of the national government under President Hipólito Yrigoyen in breaking the power structure which had been in force prior to implementation of the Sáenz Peña Law in Córdoba; had these not been the causes, the national and international repercussions of this student movement would not be comprehensible. The power structure of Córdoba had to accommodate itself to the national power structure.

According to reports of the time by participants in the reformist movement and scholars of the university reform of Córdoba, the reformist movement had much to do with the function the Cordobese aristocracy discharged in the power structure, and certainly relating not merely to the University.[1] This is clearly inferred from the reform manifesto of 1918 which, in spite of being directed to all of Latin America, refers—perhaps as a typical indication of the entire Latin

14

American situation—especially to the Córdoba case.[2] All the works which have studied and analyzed the phenomenon of the university reform of 1918, be they in defense or critical, have in one way or another alluded to these circumstances.[3] Historical analysis of this epoch also brought out this point.

It is not our present intent to analyze and study the university reform, but rather to show the importance of this institution to the stability of the aristocracy as the ruling social stratum of Córdoba, which besides its specific functions, was a fount of work for the Cordobese aristocracy and was a control mechanism of the ruling elites who could take part in the power structure. The University as an institution had great influence on getting things done in Córdoba. In a more or less similar form, this is seen in the investigation which served as basis for the present work.[4] Therein, it could be seen that the University, as an institutional sector participating in community decisions, had more influence around 1940 (approximately) than around 1963 (approximately); the functions of the University in the power structure of Córdoba, it seemed, tended to diminish as those of other institutional sectors tied to the process of industrial development increased. Thus, from occupying second place around 1940, in an order of influence relative to community action, it went to seventh place around 1963.[5] And in the past, the situation could not have been much different, at least if we are guided by documents of the time and by the opinions of authors and historians at the beginning of the century.[6] Sarmiento, towards the middle of the 19th century, in his *Facundo,* attacked the importance of the University of Córdoba with harsh and critical words. Nonetheless, one must not overlook the social function of the University in the structure of Córdoba at the beginning of the century: the preparation of the ruling elites and their selective control. This function is of vital importance to the entire social stratum controlling all the power, since its existence as a "governing" stratum depends upon the role its ruling elites fulfill within the power structure. The university reform—perhaps without these ruling reformists having proposed it—signified the possibility of creation of institutionalized mechanisms for the formation of new ruling elites, which could place the stability of the Cordobese power elite in jeopardy and, along with this, the possibility of the Cordobese aristocracy gradually losing control of the power structure. Therefore, our working definition of the Cordobese aristocracy refers to the social stratum which controls the power prior to 1918 through the ruling elites representing it. Thus, we eliminate the difficult problem of the definition of an aristocracy and of its characteristic criteria; a problem which, on the other hand, is not resolved in the theoretical field.[8]

      TWO We now would like to answer the following questions: what is the Cordobese aristocracy like?, what are its characteristics?, on what does it base its power and its superiority over the common people?; and finally, what was the social stratification before 1918? We will base our replies on documents of the time and descriptions by writers of the social life of Córdoba in the early years of the present century. The description of Cordobese aristocracy before 1918 will serve as the definition of the aristocracy throughout this volume.

According to documents of the day, newspaper accounts, and some special works, the social stratification before 1918 consisted of a system of vertical ordination of the population on the basis of power relationships, in the broadest sense. The occupations of the citizens of Córdoba ordered these power relationships and, therefore, a prestige scale was established of these occupations to which the members of the different social strata had access. The performance of the occupational roles fixed the status of the people, who arranged themselves into social strata. Access to occupational roles depended upon several factors, some being appointive and others acquisitive for the individuals involved. This fact made the social strata into more or less closed or open arrangements, according to the preeminence of these factors. To a large degree it corresponded to an estate type of system, inasmuch as there was a family preference for access to the higher estates with certain institutionalized channels of vertical mobility. A description of the different estates (or social strata) will establish their functionality within the system, since each one has distinct social functions in the community structure.[)]

1. At the highest part of the pyramid of occupational prestige one found a *doctoral aristocracy* composed of "doctors, licenciados, masters, and bachelors of the Casa de Trejo."[10] Basically, they were lawyers, doctors, engineers, and clerks of the high court of justice (and perhaps some theologians or ranking priests) who practiced their liberal profession and occupied the high posts of the government, the official bureaucracy, the University, and the law. The exercise of their university professions conferred upon them a high status and a great social prestige which made them available for access to the highest honors. The most "select" by virtue of their capability or professional talents formed the ruling elites of that aristocracy in the different institutional sectors of community life. As such, they were "the trustees of all the knowledge of the age"[11] within the area which prescribed their concept of life and a scholastic or liberal philosophy based on religious and moral values. The less select members of this doctoral aristocracy occupied the lesser ranks in the function of government; they were the functionaries of the ministries, of the municipality, of banks, etc.

The distribution of offices in the bureaucracy depended on the ruling elites (the political leaders) and the area of influence in which they moved. Personal relationships, based on friendship and kinship, built up informal groups—often opposing amongst themselves—which, according to the success of the "leaders" in the political arena, determined the distribution of offices within the in-group. The influence of national leaders (Roca, Juárez Celman, Figueroa Alcorta, Cárcano, etc.) was decisive in forming these groups (Roquistas, Juaristas, etc.) and the power struggle of these groups was wont to be extremely violent. These groups arose within this self-same doctoral aristocracy, whose governing function was never for a moment in doubt, since it was "a free and universally respected aristocracy" whose claim to the exercise of the governing function was based on its well-known "superiority over the common people"[12] bestowed by the aura of the Colony which "resisted the levelling commotions of the Independence."[13]

Some members (and not many) of this doctoral aristocracy reinforced their power (although not their prestige) with a certain control of the economic life in that they owned lands (especially in the northern and western parts of the Province) or urban and suburban property in the City. According to records of the time, they were few, and their economic basis was not very strong. The economic power of this doctoral aristocracy was based on the exercise of the liberal professions and in the office of public administration. Consequently—and certainly within a minimally diversified economy—the economic capacity of this doctoral aristocracy was very limited, and luxury and economic ostentation were confined to a very few persons (or families). Therefore, the life-style of this doctoral aristocracy was more showy and formalistic than luxurious and ostentatious. This caused this aristocracy to justify its way of life with a refinement in the forms of manners and dress and great adherence to "the old customs, without changing their ancient splendor"; erudition, manner of speech, and the art of conversation were esteemed.

The social life of the doctoral aristocracy was ruled by a fixed family life in which the wife carried out a decisive role in the social development and education of the offspring within the social and moral norms determined by esteem for the religious and moral values above all others.[14] Veneration of the family name dated from the great political, social, and cultural events of the colony, the independence and the period of *caudillismo* and national organization; the founders of the country were affected by it. The great social esteem implied by the doctoral parchment, the doctor's tassels, allowed access to this aristocracy to persons not connected to those events of the past or by family name; therefore, precisely, that which basically defined this aristocracy was its "doctoral" character which allowed it access to high rank and marriage. This mechanism of access to the aristocracy allowed it to retain an internal cohesiveness, based on acquired characteristics such as the doctoral parchment, which permitted it to stay in control of the community power structure for a long time, resisting the levelling influences of the independence, liberalism, and the until then incipient foreign immigration. This doctoral character of the Cordobese aristocracy is what justified its superiority over the common people and control of all the power, since all the ruling elites could represent this doctoral aristocracy within the traditional structure of society of that time.[15]

2. At a lower prestige level, and almost constituting a separate sphere, but very closely tied to the doctoral aristocracy, were the estancieros, who were masters over "boundless dominions" (particularly in the northern, central, and western regions of the Province of Córdoba), usually inherited from the times of colonizing, the independence and conquest of the desert. They were "industrious and dedicated"[16] to the demands of the land and possessed more a spirit of patronage than profit. The holdings were worked in the old way with more common sense and actual experience than wisdom; they were small feudal realms with a very characteristic system of social relationships in which the *patron* was the source of all decisions; responsibilites and mutual rights bound together all the workers on an estancia,

from the family of the patrón to the families of the laborers.
Life on the estancias was normally hard and unadorned;
the heads of the estancias responded more to necessities of
country life than to possibilities of a refined life. They were
normally "unlearned, vigorous and strong" and were
satisfied "with their routine and their ignorance."[17] The life-
style was simple and at times very primitive. The isolation
contributed to family customs—perhaps in veneration of the
old caudillos—following gaucho and folklore traditions,
especially regarding food, clothing, language, and domestic
and rural customs. The estancieros—or members of their
family—sometimes made excursions into politics by holding
provincial senatorships of the Departments in which their
lands were situated; they played a decisive role in electoral
struggles, since they controlled the decisions of their own
staff and those of the local people by virtue of their prestige
as *patrón*. Upon reaching a certain age the estancieros retired
to Córdoba—which was when they showed up—"to rest in
the years of old age" or to secure "a good match for their
daughter and doctoral tassels or a high post for their son."[18]
We say they almost constituted a separate estate because
frequently the rough manners of the estancieros collided with
"the fine courteous manners" which the doctoral aristocracy
cultivated and with the "prescribed" ritualism of social
activity found in the home life and in the "clubs" (El Panal,
the Club Social).[19] The estanciero's wife was the connecting
link to the doctoral aristocracy, since it was she who
maintained the ascetic and formalistic atmosphere of which
Sarmiento spoke.[20] The economic support provided by his
domains often allowed the estanciero to lead an ostentatious
and expensive life, making him forget the "dark shade of his
skin" brought from the Colony or the rough country life.
Cultivation of current moral and religious values made him
similar to the "haughty doctors of the City."
   3. Next, and perhaps very close to the above, although
constituting an intermediate stratum, were found the

pelucones, "curious incarnation of the spirit of so much per cent."[21] They were essentially merchants (cloth, hats, tobacco, foodstuffs, owners of hide and pelt warehouses, or of some grain-mill or beverage factory); many of them (the majority) were of foreign origin, particularly Spanish, Italian, or French, coming to the City at the end of the 19th century. In their commercial profession they were "very honest and successful enough, neither passive nor aggressive, strict fathers and indifferent citizens."[22] They formed an intermediate stratum, certainly smaller, between the doctoral aristocracy and the estancieros on the one hand, and the rest of the populace on the other.

The pelucones controlled the commercial life of the City and if, in the beginning, they did not have enough capital, they slowly learned how to accumulate it. They are the founders of a commercial bourgeois which laid claim to its power by the accumulation of capital savings which, thanks to a sobriety of life and control of expenditures, slowly grew. They neither made nor were interested in a show of money; they were engaged solely in expanding their "business" at the cost of working and saving and buying property, especially urban. Commercial success allowed them to ascend to the same doctoral aristocracy through their sons, who customarily undertook the *rites of passage* of university studies. The sons of the pelucones were brought up in a strict family morality and with great emphasis on the value of formal education, especially the university career. Therefore, according to the rules of the game imposed by the doctoral aristocracy, they were always prepared to ascend to it through marriage.

4. At the lowest level of the pyramid of social prestige one found the plebeian masses who performed all the other functions of community life, from the low bureaucratic posts in provincial or municipal administration to service duties. They formed the working hand of the community which, through having a very limited economy—almost that of

subsistence level—limited manual occupations to certain sectors (clerks in shops or warehouses, construction, workers in some small factory, porters, artisans, etc.). The artisans and small independent merchants were the most respected within this stratum, as well as the clerks of large stores or State employees.

This entire range of occupations was grouped within a single stratum, since vertical mobility upwards to another level was rare. Records indicate that, copying the doctoral aristocracy, the members of this stratum were wont to assume a doctoral air; from this was coined the saying: "Once there was a Cordobese who was not a doctor." They were very deferential to their situation which they respected with a "natural" submission to their social inferiority as compared to the "fine people."

According to reports, at the beginning of the century "the brown and Chinese (Indian) races were already on the wane and native peasants were increasing,"[23] coming in from the country with the first processes of urbanization of the City, which begin, perhaps, around 1880. Statistics of the 1895 and 1914 censuses bear this out.[24] They formed the bulk of the population, possessed a very low standard of living, a limited economic capacity, little or no education, and were concentrated in specific areas of the city (Upper Córdoba, San Vincente, La Toma, San Martín, etc.). They were generally hard-working and honest, which distinguished them from the rabble or marginals (vagabonds, rogues, prostitutes, etc.) who were confined to specific well-known "redoubtable" enclaves of the City. Certain moral virtues and personal conditions made them available for some mixing (or patronage) which permitted them to ascend the social scale through the institutionalized way of formal education, and in some cases they reached the doctoral aristocracy.

THREE "At the beginning of this century

Cordobese society could still be described as being saturated with aristocratic customs, formalist ritualism, and attachment to the parchment, within an atmosphere dominated by the prestige of the university diploma and by the respectable figures of the pelucón (an expression of high commerce) and the estanciero."[25] This picture began to change "when the immigrant population, little by little abandoning rural isolation, mixed its sons with the half native and took on functions primarily in politics and city commerce."[26] This began to occur in the first two decades of this century when the opportunity arose for the sons of the immigrants, particularly Italian and Spanish, to participate in political issues with the rise to power of the Radical Civic Union (1916) and the university reform of 1918, since they relied upon the institutionalized mechanisms for the formation of ruling elites which would represent other social strata and not only the Cordobese aristocracy.

The Spanish and Italian immigrations in the last decades of the 19th century became manifested in Córdoba through the sons, that is, the second generation. Economic success, particularly for those from the country, from the south and east portions of the Province, as well as the success of immigrants from other Provinces, permitted immigrants to send their sons to the City and, especially, to study in the University. The institutionalized mechanism for social ascension in Córdoba was the University and it was available to all of these people; the size of this wave of immigrants' sons overpowered the gates manned by the Cordobese aristocracy and inundated them. University reform surged and the mechanism for preparation of new ruling elites was created. The new ideas were absorbed by the university youth—also by many members of the doctoral aristocracy or, perhaps, through having been doctoral—and the social protest movement against the power elite surged forth. Therefore, a reform in the power structure of Córdoba had to be a university reform. The doctoral aristocracy—and

with regard to the estancieros.

Nevertheless, the channel of access to the doctoral aristocracy was matrimony; the rite of passage was the university diploma, the doctor's tassels. Once this rite of passage was satisfied, it no longer made any difference about the *pelucón* or immigrant background, nor even the color of the skin, for access to marriage. The Cordobese aristocracy opened the doors of its homes only to doctors from other social strata. To a certain extent, a matrilineal lineage was created. On this account, the Cordobese woman of the aristocracy will be a decisive factor in access to it and, therefore, "new" conditions were imposed: "fine courteous manners" and, above all, "a pure family and moral life." This woman was "pompous and formalistic, cultivated and devout," who esteemed, above all others, the "moral and religious" values.[32] The pelucones—according to records of the time—had a very strict family morality and, therefore, the doors of access to the aristocracy were always open to them.

Through what has been said it can be inferred that there were two gates controlling the institutionalized way of access to the Cordobese aristocracy and, therefore, they are the characteristics which define it as a social stratum (and both are acquired): on one hand, the university diploma and, on the other, the pure social and moral life; the first was controlled by the doctors of the Casa de Trejo, and the second by the women and their allies: the clergy. In the following pages we will try to see the destiny of this doctoral aristocracy across fifty years of history.

III

The Aristocracy
in Power

ONE In this study only certain institutional positions of power during the years 1924, 1937, 1951, and 1960 are considered; in them, the ruling elites are placed (visibly). Furthermore, this present investigation of the power structure does not claim to be exhaustive, since the invisible leaders who have so much influence in the decisions of these same ruling elites are lacking. The limitations of our analysis have two causes: (1) the fact of only considering the institutional government positions with reference to the Executive Power (governors, vice-governors, ministers, and chief of police, as well as the municipal administrator of the City); the Legislative Power (National senators, National deputies, and Provincial senators); and the Judicial Power (Superior Court of Justice and its members); also considered are the high offices of the University government (rector, vice-rector, and deans); and some national government offices (ministers etc.); and (2) the fact of considering only the key years (whose justification is given in the explanation of the methodology used in this work) corresponding to four historical periods which embrace almost fifty years of political life of the City of Córdoba. Since our objective is to observe a trend, we believe the stated limitations can be justified, since our investigation is significant enough to comprehend the political ruling elites.

Also, and to avoid misunderstandings—although it seems

obvious enough—it must be pointed out that these institutional positions, as regards the availability of offices, are very different in each of the historical periods concerned, since parallel to development of the community an increase in these institutional positions is produced. This is seen—and, certainly, it is very logical—in all the sectors studied: the provincial ministers, national deputies, provincial senators, members of the supreme council, deans, rectors (with the new universities), etc., all increase. This necessitates analyzing the participation of the Cordobese aristocracy in the power structure of the city through percentages of availability of the institutional positions. The appraisal of the availability of institutional positions and of participation by the ruling elites of the Cordobese aristocracy in them certainly tends to be indicative of a situation or a trend.

The last explanation we wish to make is that often the figures given for institutional positions are more than really exist. This is owing to the fact that at times—for electoral reasons, for example—two persons have held the same position in the same year. This happened primarily with the Judiciary in 1924, since the Superior Court of Justice was created in that year and some members of the supreme council went on to occupy those positions, or, as in 1937 with the Legislative, when up to a given moment there was one set of individuals and afterwards another, or in 1924 with the university deans, etc. In order to avoid an arbitrary choice, we have preferred to consider all persons who occupied the institutional positions in the key year, since here the exact number of institutional positions is relevant to the halves. Of real interest is the participation of the Cordobese aristocracy in these positions, although it can vary by a small percentage. In all, what is important is the trend which becomes clearly apparent through having such a long pause between periods. We do not want these limitations of a methodological nature, in this empirical study, to pass without being brought to attention.

TWO The availability of institutional positions analyzed in our work, distributed by sectors and historical periods, is as follows:

1924:	1) Political sector		46
	2) Judicial sector		12
	3) University sector		4
		Total:	62
1937:	1) Political sector		60
	2) Judicial sector		14
	3) University sector		4
		Total:	78
1951:	1) Political sector		57
	2) Judicial sector		35
	3) University sector		9
		Total:	101
1960:	1) Political sector		71
	2) Judicial sector		43
	3) University sector		18
		Total:	132

The increases in positions in these periods are due to very different reasons ranging, for example, from the newly created labor councils in the third period or of the Catholic University of Córdoba in the fourth period, to the increase of provincial ministries through technical necessities, of national deputies through increase in population, and provincial senators through formation of new Departments. Furthermore, the fact of only an increase in positions implies a development of the power structure of Córdoba, as much due to technical reasons connected to the new forms of government as for reasons of service needs tied to the increase in population. This fact has great importance for the subject of our study, since it proves the impossibility for one social stratum (if one wishes, closed) to satisfy all the requirements of the function of government.

The participation of the ruling elites of the Cordobese aristocracy in the institutional positions given in our example, and also distributed by periods and sectors, is as follows:

1924:	1) Political sector	31
	2) Judicial sector	12
	3) University sector	5
		—
	Total:	48
1937:	1) Political sector	28
	2) Judicial sector	13
	3) University sector	4
		—
	Total:	45
1951:	1) Political sector	9
	2) Judicial sector	25
	3) University sector	2
		—
	Total:	36
1960:	1) Political sector	5
	2) Judicial sector	21
	3) University sector	11
		—
	Total:	37

The data presented here immediately show how participation of the ruling elites of the Cordobese aristocracy in the power structure of the city—defined by the institutional positions chosen for this study—apparently tends to diminish, since the percentages of participation compared to the availability of institutional positions is as follows:

1924:	77.4%	1951:	35.6%
1937:	57.7%	1960:	28.1%

The most notable fact about this gradual decline of participation by the ruling elites of the Cordobese aristocracy in the power structure of the city is the levelling-off of participation—within the gradual diminishing process—in the fourth period (1960), since after following a more or less regular rhythm (approximately 20 and 22 percent) between the first and second period and the second and third period, it goes to 7 percent. This fact must have a certain relevance, particularly if our working hypothesis and the independent variable which we use in the investigation are taken into account, because it coincides with the beginning of the process of industrial development of the city (around 1955). And here the participation of the ruling elites of the Cordobese aristocracy in the power structure can denote representation of other sectors—and not that of its own social stratum—or a modification in the internal structure of this same Cordobese aristocracy. (We shall return to this later.)

If some general conclusion can be drawn from this first approach to the bulk figures, it is that as the community develops (through increase in population, industrial development, complexity of the function of government, etc.)—that is, as it modernizes—it would appear that the Cordobese aristocracy becomes less important in decisions taken in the community because its ruling elites diminish and tend to withdraw into certain institutional sectors (the law, for example). From this, it would seem that as the aristocracy becomes less important in decisions taken in the community, it tends to appear as more residual in the power structure in the face of the process of development.[1] And this means a gradual margination from the process defining the decisions taken in Córdoba by the aristocracy as a social stratum, since its ruling elites share control of the power structure with other ruling elites.

Nevertheless, whatever may be the value of this tendency towards a decrease in participation by the Cordobese aristocracy in the power structure of the city, it is of note that this aristocracy still numbers a very high percentage[2] compared to what occurs in other more developed societies. This implies a certain permanence in the power structure of the city by the ruling elites of the Cordobese aristocracy and which—as already pointed out—we had discovered in an investigation carried out earlier.[3] Without a doubt, the internal structure of this aristocracy must play a very important role here, which, as we said, tended to define itself by its doctoral character. Nonetheless, in order to analyze this structure, we must first ascertain the sectoral distribution of the participation of these ruling elites in the institutionalized power structure. By sectors and periods, participation of the Cordobese aristocracy is:

1924:	1) Political sector	67.3%
	2) Judicial sector	100.0%
	3) University sector	100.0%
1937:	1) Political sector	36.7%
	2) Judicial sector	93.0%
	3) University sector	100.0%
1951:	1) Political sector	15.8%
	2) Judicial sector	71.4%
	3) University sector	22.3%
1960:	1) Political sector	7.0%
	2) Judicial sector	48.8%
	3) University sector	61.1%

In general, the first thing these data show is the tendency of the ruling elites of the Cordobese aristocracy to concentrate in certain sectors as it loses influence in its participation in the city's power structure. From all indications, the sector which shows the most marked tendency of this loss of influence is the political sector. In the third period (1951) its participation is slight (15.8%), and in the fourth (1960) it is already irrelevant (7.0%); in the first and second periods (1924 and 1937), on the contrary, it is markedly significant (67.3% and 36.7%), since it must be taken into consideration that in these periods the distribution of political offices was largely (almost entirely) between two political parties: the Democratic Party and the Radical Party. In 1924 the National Government was Radical, and the Provincial Government was Democratic; and in 1937, to the contrary, the National Government was Democratic (Conservative), and the Provincial Government was Radical. Therefore, it is clear that the political-party variable is significant in determining the participation of the ruling elites of the Cordobese aristocracy in the power structure of the city. This fact becomes even more evident when one sees that in 1951 both the National and Provincial Governments were Peronista, and in 1960 both were Desarollista (UCRI).

Naturally, all of these elements must be more carefully analyzed; this we will do later when we consider the ideology of the ruling elites of the Cordobese aristocracy. In any event, the relationship among participation in political parties, ideology, and aristocracy seems to be significant in determining the participation of the Cordobese aristocracy in the power structure when referring to the political sector. The importance of this derives from the fact that prior to 1918 the Cordobese aristocracy seemed to possess, almost by inherent right (natural?), the exercise of the function of government in a manner "universally acknowledged" owing to its "well-known superiority over the common people."[4] And this would mean, in the face of the raw statistics, the political eclipse of the aristocracy. We will return to this later in more detail.

To the contrary, the judicial and university sectors show a greater permanency within a declining trend of participation by the aristocracy. In the judicial sector it goes from controlling 100% of the available positions in 1924 to

controlling almost 50% in 1960. In the first place, these
percentages are very significant because they surpass by far
the percentages of means of participation by the Cordobese
aristocracy in the power structure analyzed in this study.
Thus, we have:

1924: judicial sector:	100%	- total:	77.4%
1937: judicial sector:	93%	- total:	57.7%
1951: judicial sector:	71%	- total:	35.6%
1960: judicial sector:	49%	- total:	28.1%

And in the second place, these percentages are very
significant because one must consider the variables of the
development of the available positions, the growth in
population, and the process of industrial development with
all its implications regarding the quantitative proportion of
the aristocracy with respect to the total population of
Córdoba as shown by the censuses.

In the university sector, nevertheless, there is a variable
which influences the third period (1951), since it is the only
period in which the percentage of participation by the
Cordobese aristocracy in this sector declines with respect to
the total percentage and means of participation in the power
structure analyzed in this study. And this variable can only be
ideology. The statistics give the following figures:

1924: university sector:	100.0%	- total:	77.4%
1937: university sector:	100.0%	- total:	57.7%
1951: university sector:	22.3%	- total:	35.6%
1960: university sector:	61.1%	- total:	28.1%

One must not forget that the third period was controlled by
Peronismo, and for the first time the National Government
interfered at the National University of Córdoba and cast out
its professors. In the fourth period (1960) one sees a marked
resurgence owing to the presence of the Catholic University
of Córdoba, which absorbed a large number of professors of

the aristocracy in the first years of its creation (1958). One must not forget that our sample, with respect to the university sector, refers only to the directorate of the university who, in principle, cannot be considered a true picture of the body of professors; nevertheless, some halo of prestige must attach to these aristocrats, since they occupy directoral posts. And this, to a large degree, is very significant for reasons we shall give later, and in part, owing to the characteristics of the Cordobese aristocracy which we pointed out in the previous chapter.

THREE The facts presented tend to show a trend of diminishing participation in the power structure of the city by the ruling elites of the Cordobese aristocracy. However, this tendency towards decline has certain special characteristics. For the moment, and in general, this tendency towards decline is not so significant in the judicial and university sectors; to the contrary, one notes within the tendency a certain permanency of the aristocracy in these sectors, above all if compared to what happens in the political sector. To go from 100% to 61.1% (disregarding the third period) in the university sector and from 100% to 48.8% in the judicial sector is a fairly relative declining tendency, taking into account the development of the community. It would seem as if the Cordobese aristocracy had a certain predilection for these institutional sectors. Although we have no definite figures (since these were not the object of this investigation) on the percentage of members of the Cordobese aristocracy who practice their liberal professions and who occupy significant posts in private institutions and agencies (professional associations, important private clinics, construction firms, factories, consultants, etc.) and in public institutions and agencies (banks, Departments, hospitals, etc.), according to approximate figures obtained in another, earlier, investigation, the percentage of university professionals who are members of the Cordobese aristocracy is fairly high.[5] All these facts make it evident that a certain university professional tradition (doctorates) has been maintained within the Cordobese aristocracy and that this fact, to a great extent, determines its availability for participation in the city power structure. In the previous study on the power structure of Córdoba, one could see the high percentage of university professionals among the top influentials and key influentials of the community, among whom one found many members of the Cordobese aristocracy.[6] These percentages were much higher than those found in the other cities studied. Only insofar as there exists a large availability of university professionals—in this instance we refer almost exclusively to lawyers—among the members of the Cordobese aristocracy, can one explain the high percentage of participation in posts (judicial and university) which inexorably require a university degree.

The concentration shown by the Cordobese aristocracy on certain institutional sectors such as Judicial, University, and the Liberal Professions to a great extent continues the doctoral tradition which had characterized it before 1918; it would seem that the exercise of university professions is the source of activity of the Cordobese aristocracy and that which allows it to remain (relatively) in the power structure of Córdoba. Therefore, it means that the Cordobese aristocracy forms its ruling elites in the University and that these ruling elites (universitarians) are the ones who keep this social strata at the level of prestige in which, one could almost say, it has always been found. The exercise of this university-gained advantage in the Judicial, University, and Liberal Professions gives the members of the Cordobese aristocracy the high status they enjoy in the community and, perhaps, beyond it.

FOUR Below is an analysis of the university degrees possessed by the members of the Cordobese aristocracy who participate in the city power structure which we have analyzed in this work, distributed by periods and type of degree.

TABLE I

		1st period		2nd period		3rd period		4th period	
c	Degree	No.	%	No.	%	No.	%	No.	%
a	Lawyer - Court Clerk	31	65	30	66	34	95	30	81
b	Doctor - dentist	7	15	9	20	2	5	5	14
c	Engineer - architect	4	8	3	7	0	0	2	5
e	No degree	3	6	3	7	0	0	0	0
d	Military - journalistic	3	6	0	0	0	0	0	0
	Totals:	48	100	45	100	36	100	37	100

The first thing one notices in Table I is the high percentage of lawyers-clerks in all periods. This fact is perfectly logical when one takes into account the institutional sectors considered in this study: judicial and, in part, the university and politics. In order to avoid the enormous weight of the lawyers-clerks who principally are concentrated in the judicial sector and partly in the university sector, we will analyze only the political sector to see if there exists the same professional tradition among members of the Cordobese aristocracy who participate in the power structure of the city. The ruling elites of the Cordobese aristocracy who have had functions in the city power structure in the political sector and who possess a university degree represent, in the four periods:

in 1924:   80.7%   in 1951:   100.0%
in 1937:   89.3%   in 1960:   100.0%

The mere display of these percentages clearly shows the university preparation of the ruling elites of the Cordobese aristocracy also for the political sector. And further: these percentages could reach a 100% absolute in all the periods if one excludes the Provincial senators from functions in the political sector since—as we have shown earlier—to a certain extent they were represented by the estancieros and not by the doctoral aristocracy of the city, estancieros who participated in the power structure during the first two periods by virtue of being caudillos of certain Departments. With only very rare exception, the political ruling elites of the Cordobese aristocracy (disregarding the Provincial senators) were from the university or were professionals; it would seem that a *conditio sine qua non* for discharging the duties of governor, ministers, national deputies, and national senators was possession of a university diploma (the doctoral parchment). Later we will analyze these facts in more detail.

For the moment, we would merely like to point out the importance a university diploma has for the ruling elites (also political) of the Cordobese aristocracy in order to participate in the power structure of the city. With it, an old tradition continued: that of being a *doctoral aristocracy,* an aristocracy dominated and ruled by the prestige of the university diploma, the doctoral parchment. Perhaps in this is found the key to its duration in the power structure of the city and its relative strength as a social stratum. This doctoral or professional tradition of the ruling elites of the Cordobese aristocracy must represent the entire social stratum and make it one always available for access to power through the prestige which the university career bestows. The university diploma is perhaps the most important characteristic of the Cordobese aristocracy. Nevertheless, its functions in the power structure of the city have been variable and continually decreasing, as we have previously noted. And this indicates that those functions in the power structure must come from structural considerations of the community and, perhaps, characteristics peculiar to this aristocracy in each of the historical periods. If the doctoral parchment appears to be a permanent characteristic, other variables must bring on the eclipse of the Cordobese aristocracy from the power structure of the city. And this is what we shall analyze in the following chapters.

IV

Family Tradition

ONE When speaking of the aristocracy, one normally tends to identify this social stratum by a series of families (or family names) which, for one reason or another, have in the past taken part in the power structure. Evidently certain families (identified by their name) make up the social stratum, especially when talking about an aristocracy; to a certain degree it follows the pattern of the nobility. But also, as in the nobility, certain families (or names) were "made" by the social stratum; they are the results of the so-called "social advancement." In the particular case of Córdoba, a certain group of families (names), very closely tied to the times of the Colony, the Independence, Caudillismo, and the national organization, and which to a certain extent played a decisive role in these historical events, forms the nucleus of the so-called Cordobese aristocracy; nevertheless, this aristocracy—which certainly was not formalized, for example, with the noble title—aristocratized other families (or names) coming from elsewhere, from abroad, or other provinces, or other social strata (pelucones, bourgeois, etc.). Certainly its number—and it could not be otherwise—was always small, although not insignificant. Important in this case are the characteristics which had to be present for access to this social stratum. The basic institutionalized channel was matrimony (although it was not the only one); hence, what is really important is to know the conditions demanded by the

Cordobese aristocracy to enter into marriage with a member of this social stratum. These conditions for entry into marriage to a great extent define this very social stratum, since they remind one of the reason for the position the stratum occupies in the social stratification system. An heroic deed, for example, enabled the hero to receive the thanks of the King by means of a noble title, and therefore, formal recognition of a new status and participation with full rights in the new estate, the nobility. In this case, the heroic deed is what defines nobility, since it is based as a social stratum on this fact. In our case, one could apply the same criterion, that is, to ascertain what conditions the aristocracy requires for marriage (the heroic deed!) of a person not belonging to that stratum, so that one becomes prepared for access to the aristocracy. We will analyze the Cordobese aristocracy from this perspective; therefore, below, we will look into the birthplace of the members of the Cordobese aristocracy who participate in the power of Córdoba, the origin of their parents, and their profession, to discover which criteria exist for admitting those from other factions or other social strata (defined by their occupation); as a result, one will be able to define the Cordobese aristocracy and, at the same time, note the changes the criteria undergo and consequently its structural changes. Finally, from this analysis we shall see which are the constants and variables defining the Cordobese aristocracy; and we will analyze this through its ruling elites, that is, individuals who have participated in the power structure for almost fifty years. Our point of reference will be the doctoral aristocracy, which serves as our definition for the Cordobese aristocracy.

TWO The birthplace of the members of the Cordobese aristocracy who took part in the community power structure in the four historical periods analyzed in this study, as well as that of their wives, shows that the Cordobese aristocracy has bonds and connections with the aristocracies of other provinces and of Buenos Aires. Even though the percentages are not very great—taking into account the singular nature of a provincial aristocracy—we feel they are still significant. Normally, aristocracies of different provinces tend to form ties among themselves. The figures representing the Cordobese aristocracy have the characteristic of increased ties with Buenos Aires in the second and third period, and particularly among the ruling elites of the Cordobese aristocracy who participated in the power in the national order and in the political sector. The percentages of members of the Cordobese aristocracy married to women from other provinces and from Buenos Aires, by periods, are as follows:

| 1924: | 12% | 1951: | 17% |
| 1937: | 17% | 1960: | 8% |

These figures are interesting if compared with the percentages of members of the Cordobese aristocracy born in other provinces and in Buenos Aires—although they are settled in Córdoba—since it would seem that in the Cordobese aristocracy the fact that the husband be Cordobese took precedence. The figures are the following, by historical periods:

| 1924: | 8% | 1951: | 9% |
| 1937: | 13% | 1960: | 8% |

The place of family residence, doubtless determined by the home of the husband, plays an important role. Nonetheless, it is surprising that in a place like Córdoba, with its university, the home of the husband and not of the wife was more important, since she could succeed in having her husband pursue his profession in Córdoba, which, in principle, is more important than other provincial capitals. Therefore, it follows that a general criterion is the home of the husband.

The Cordobese aristocracy is linked to those of other provinces and Buenos Aires; the frequencies of linkage are significant. The provinces with which the Cordobese aristocracy is most frequently connected are: Tucumán, Santiago del Estero, La Rioja, Salta, San Juan, Santa Fe, and Corrientes. It must be observed that this linking of the Cordobese aristocracy to those of other provinces involves precisely the oldest provinces of the country, whose aristocracy is perhaps better known to the people of Córdoba.

Many of these ties come, on the one hand, through summer tourism to the mountains of Córdoba by members of the aristocracy from other provinces, and, on the other hand, through the influence of the National University of Córdoba. This fact becomes evident when one sees that the members of the Cordobese aristocracy born in other provinces or in Buenos Aires, to an overwhelming majority, have studied in the National University of Córdoba and have then remained to pursue their career in Córdoba and to marry a Cordobese woman. The University, to some extent, is a center of attraction for the aristocracies of other provinces, although not from Buenos Aires, since very few of those born there have become part of the ruling elites of the Cordobese aristocracy. Logically, Buenos Aires has always been a kind of mecca for the aristocracies of other provinces (Tucumán, Salta, etc.). In our case, this fact has a certain significance in that most of the Cordobese who married porteñas [girls of Buenos Aires] have eventually settled in Buenos Aires; and certainly, serving as national deputy, national minister, and particularly as national senator (a nine year term!) has been the springboard for settling in the federal capital.

The figures given in Table II also indicate the urban state of the Cordobese aristocracy, which tends to increase with the passing of years and shows a tendency for the wives to be more urban. The percentages, by period and by husband and wife, with respect to those born in the province of Córdoba, are as follows:

TABLE II

Place of Birth	1st period				2nd period				3rd period				4th period			
	Husband		Wife		Husband		Wife		Husband		Wife		Husband		Wife	
	No.	%	No.	%	No.	%	No.	%	No.	%	No.	%	No.	%	No.	%
Córdoba	36	75	36	75	34	76	33	73	32	88	29	80	31	84	32	86
Prov. of Córdoba	8	17	3	6.25	5	11	1	2.2	1	3	0	—	2	5	1	3
Other provinces	4	8	3	6.25	5	11	2	4.5	2	6	2	6	2	5	2	5
Buenos Aires	0	—	3	6.25	1	2	6	13.3	1	3	4	11	1	3	1	3
Foreign	0	—	0	—	—	—	0	—	0	0	0	0	1	3	0	—
Unmarried	—	—	3	6.25	—	—	3	6.7	—	—	1	3	—	—	1	3
Totals:	48	100	48	100	45	100	45	100	36	100	36	100	37	100	37	100

1924:	husband:	17%		1951:	husband:	3%
	wife:	6%			wife:	0%
1937:	husband:	11%		1960:	husband:	5%
	wife:	2%			wife:	3%

This urban condition of the Cordobese aristocracy can perhaps be explained by its doctoral tradition and, to some extent, by its opposition to the estancieros. The trend shows increasing urbanization, and must relate to sources of this aristocracy's economic income. However, we do not believe this urban character of the Cordobese aristocracy is anything peculiar to it, since we presume—without positive data to that effect—that something similar must occur among the aristocracies of other provinces and Buenos Aires, although perhaps it is not a characteristic of aristocracies in other societies. Nonetheless, these data can have their importance for other characteristics which we will analyze later.

THREE Quite an important characteristic for measuring the degree of penetrability of an aristocracy is, usually, the percentage of foreigners it takes to its bosom. The criteria defining the admission of foreigners and sons of foreigners to a large extent characterize those social strata. Normally, aristocracies tend to be endogamic, that is, to recruit their members from the same social stratum; nevertheless, this never appears in absolute form. In the case of Córdoba, its aristocracy, to the contrary, has been very porous—open with respect to foreigners and sons of foreigners. Our data, referring to foreign origin of the fathers of the ruling elites of the Cordobese aristocracy, by periods, show the following:

1924:	25%	1951:	13%
1937:	25%	1960:	13%

The data and percentages are sufficiently clear to demonstrate the porosity or openness of the Cordobese aristocracy with respect to the sons of foreigners; and this is made more significant by the fact that it deals specifically with the ruling elites of that aristocracy. The percentages, particularly in the first two periods, almost lead one to suspect that national ascendancy is not necessary for belonging to the Cordobese aristocracy. Perhaps here one must consider the era: it was a question of the sons of foreigners who came into the country before 1880, that is, before the great waves of immigration. And perhaps this fact explains the later decrease, although in no case is the percentage low, at least when compared to the situation elsewhere. In general, the following conclusion could be drawn: before the immigratory waves the foreigner coming to Córdoba could have access to the aristocracy (if meeting certain conditions, to be sure); later it became more difficult. Elements of social psychology play an important role here and can lead to the corresponding explanation; but certain structural elements (immigration as such, and its prestige) and certain personal elements (level of education, manners, etc.) also play an important role.

The percentages of foreign-born mothers of members of the ruling elites of the Cordobese aristocracy have another profile. Distributed by periods, they are:

1924:	4%	1951:	2%
1937:	2%	1960:	2%

Comparing both tables and their percentages, perhaps they are directly tied to the percentages of the male and female immigration. However, worth noting is: the husbands of the foreign mothers were almost entirely not foreign; and the same occurs in reverse. Therefore, it is seen that to enter into the aristocracy the foreigner had to be married to a member of the aristocracy. With respect also to the sons of foreigners, this condition - although to a lesser extent - was in general required for entry into the aristocracy. Matrimony is the recognized and institutionalized way of access to the aristocracy; although, this way, as we have seen, was not limited.

The foreign origin of the fathers of ruling elites of the Cordobese aristocracy, by nationality and historical period, is shown in Table III.

The first notable point in Table III is the predominance of fathers of Spanish origin and the small percentage of fathers who are of neither Spanish nor Italian origin. But the really significant fact of this table is that the percentages of members of the ruling elites of the Cordobese aristocracy having fathers of Italian origin remains more or less constant through all the periods; therefore, one must question the notion (perhaps very widespread) that the sons of Italian immigrants—owing to the mass and type of the immigrants—would have more difficulties in entering the aristocracy. The figures show us that, in the four periods, 6%, 8%, 5% and 5% of the family names of the ruling elites of the Cordobese aristocracy are of Italian origin. After analyzing these figures, it cannot be maintained that, after the massive Italian immigration, a prejudice against Italian surnames existed among the Cordobese aristocracy.

FOUR The figures we have on the occupations of the fathers of the ruling elites of the Cordobese aristocracy can give us a picture a) of the occupational origin of the Cordobese aristocracy and b) of the degree of access for people coming from lower social strata, that is, on the percentage of social advancement into the aristocracy. These figures are extremely important for understanding the texture of the Cordobese aristocracy. The figures, by period and occupation, are shown in Table IV:

TABLE III

	Origin of parents	1st period				2nd period				3rd period				4th period			
		Father		Mother		Father		Mother		Father		Mother		Father		Mother	
		No.	%	No.	%	No.	%	No.	%	No.	%	No.	%	No.	%	No.	%
a	Argentina or Latin America	36	75	46	96	33	74	44	98	31	87	35	98	32	87	36	98
b	Spain	7	15	1	2	5	11	0	—	3	8	0	—	3	8	1	2
c	Italy	3	6	0	—	4	9	0	—	2	5	1	2	2	5	0	—
d	Elsewhere	2	4	1	2	3	6	1	2	0	—	0	—	0	—	0	—
	Totals:	48	100	48	100	45	100	45	100	36	100	36	100	37	100	37	100

TABLE IV

		1st period		2nd period		3rd period		4th period	
c	Father's occupation	No.	%	No.	%	No.	%	No.	%
a	University profes-sional	10	21	17	38	20	56	29	78
b	Estanciero or financier	19	40	11	25	0	—	0	—
c	Military or political	3	6	1	2	0	—	0	—
d	Commerce or industry	7	15	12	27	7	19	6	16
e	Functionary or employee	4	8	2	4	9	25	2	6
f	Others (inferior type)	5	10	2	4	0	—	0	—
	Totals:	48	100	45	100	36	100	37	100

The first thing one notices in the chart is the rise, through the four periods, in members of the ruling elites of the Cordobese aristocracy descended from professional fathers, that is, with university diplomas; this becomes more significant when one notes the decrease in members of the ruling elites of the Cordobese aristocracy descended from fathers with rural or urban properties, to where in the third and fourth periods no member of the ruling elites of the aristocracy appears who is the son of an estanciero or financier. Even though this information may not mean that none of the members of the Cordobese aristocracy are descended from fathers who are estancieros or financiers, the conclusion must be drawn with benefit of inventory. Nevertheless, the figures given reveal, on the one hand, the professional tradition of the ruling elites of the Cordobese aristocracy—to the point where it increases through the years!—and, on the other, the lack of estanciera tradition of the ruling elites of the Cordobese aristocracy, especially regarding the judicial and university areas, since the numbers of members of the ruling elites of the Cordobese aristocracy with estanciero fathers appear in the first and second periods and only then in the political area, especially at the provincial level (provincial senatorships).

To the contrary, in the above figures, relatively high percentages are noticed for members of the ruling elites of the Cordobese aristocracy with fathers coming from commerce or industry. In Córdoba, this economic sector was almost entirely controlled by foreigners; therefore, the percentages tend to coincide with those obtained for members of the aristocracy who are sons of foreign fathers. Later we shall note the fact that the aristocracy, in general, has not dedicated itself to commercial and industrial activities. The sons of merchants and industrialists had no difficulties in joining the Cordobese aristocracy through marriage, since the percentages (15, 27, 19 and 16%, respectively, for each period) are relatively significant. On the other hand, the percentages show no trends, which tends to prove what was previously stated.

The decrease of the sons of military men (or politicians, although the data obtained, perhaps because of methodological deficiencies, do not convince us) among the ruling elites of the Cordobese aristocracy does not have much relevance; it would seem that in this century a military career does not attract the Cordobese aristocracy. The same could be said with respect to the sons of functionaries and employees, since they were part of the estate bureaucracy, although at a lower level. The significance of this fact as a social advance would be discovered if one knew the profession of the grandfathers, to see if it was a question, really, of a social advance. We are not inclined to say this with the data we possess, since many members of the aristocracy were estate functionaries and employees who, at that time, enjoyed a certain occupational prestige; it would have been interesting to see the rise of the functionaries and employees, that is, of the members of another social class and not of the aristocracy. The exercise of bureaucratic functions (some, certainly) does not signify a social decline.

Nevertheless, the data given with respect to the members of the ruling elites of the Cordobese aristocracy coming from fathers having other occupations of an inferior level result in quite significant disclosures, since social ascension appears in all clarity. The percentages in the four periods are the following: 10, 4, 0 and 0. It would seem that in the course of the years the Cordobese aristocracy had hardened towards the members of lower social strata. This is very significant if one recalls the porosity shown to sons of merchants or industrialists and of foreigners. Contrary to what could be foreseen, earlier there were more members of the ruling elites who came from lower social strata than at present; at least, this is what the figures indicate. It would seem that an economic "principle" begins to have importance for access to the aristocracy, since it can be supposed that those coming from fathers of lower social levels do not possess the economic backing of those coming from fathers who are merchants or industrialists. Thus, a certain change in the internal structure of the ruling elites of the Cordobese aristocracy begins to appear.

In review, the data show us, on the one hand, an increase of sons of professionals and merchants and industrialists among the ruling elites of the Cordobese aristocracy, and, on the other, a decrease in sons of members of lower social strata and a decrease in sons of estancieros or financiers. The ruling elites of the Cordobese aristocracy, therefore, tend each time to become more professional and industrial (merchants), at least, this is observed among the ruling elites of the political, judicial, and university sectors. It must be pointed out that this tendency has special relevance for the ruling elites active in the judicial and perhaps university sectors, since it is in these areas where participation of the Cordobese aristocracy in the power structure becomes increasingly evident. It would appear that, in order to be a magistrate, one must in principle be the son of a professional or, lacking this, the son of a merchant or industrialist and only as an exception the son of a functionary or employee. In any event, the professional tradition is basic and continues increasingly so with every period (20, 40, 56 and 78%, respectively). All these facts will become more significant when we analyze other variables.

V

The Sources
of Power

ONE All aristocracy, because of the place it occupies in social stratification, must justify its sources of power; among these are found, basically, the economic sources which sustain the social strata situated at the highest part of the social stratification pyramid, and according to what these sources are, so will depend the structure of this social stratum and the function it fulfills in the power structure. Normally the aristocracies have been—and are—looked upon as "rich" social strata having control of the sources of economic power of a community. It is very possible that within the social stratification system in which the aristocracies are functionally found (estate-type systems) there exists a coincidence of this social stratum with the control of the sources of economic power; but when this social stratum performs functionally in another system of social stratification (a class system, for example), it is also very possible that these factors do not coincide; and perhaps, therefore, in a community which finds itself in a process of industrial development it becomes a "residual" social stratum. In the case of Córdoba, this is a matter we will analyze later.

Nonetheless, the aristocracies, as a social stratum belonging to a social stratification system of the estate type, normally have controlled the sources of economic power in agrarian or rural societies: that is, they had the source of their economic power in the main sector of the economy: the land. In our country, in the study carried out by José Luis de Imaz on the upper class of Buenos Aires[1] and, in part, in his study on "Los Que Mandan,"[2] it was possible to verify this constant of the aristocracies. But in these same studies it was noted that the so-called "upper class of Buenos Aires" (the aristocracy) was, in fact, very closely linked to the industrial and business sectors of Buenos Aires.[3] The modern enterprises, organized under the form of anonymous societies, have enabled the aristocracies to take part in the processes of industrial development; and they formed special aristocracies—much of this has also occurred in France, Germany, England, and the United States—that base their economic power in industry. In the years studied and through what the collected data reveal to us, the Cordobese aristocracy is not similar to these types of aristocracies; it would rather seem to resemble, *mutatis mutandi,* the old dethroned nobilities of Europe, at least regarding sources of economic power.[4] Nor did the doctoral aristocracy before 1918 correspond, in general, to the customary patterns found in Argentina (Buenos Aires, Mendoza, Tucumán, Salta, Corrientes, etc.). We shall endeavor to see on what the Cordobese aristocracy bases its economic power, seen through its ruling elites who participated in the power between 1918 and 1966.

We have divided the sources of economic power into those which come from a profession and those coming from other sources (land, commerce, industry, income, property, etc.); it must not be forgotten that occupation is the means by which, sociologically, one participates in the economic system; but one can have a multi-occupationality.

TWO Tables V and VI display the data obtained regarding occupation and income of the ruling elites of the Cordobese aristocracy.

TABLE V

1st period

Occupation and Income	O Professional income	X Farm	Y Commerce and industry	Z Income property	XZ Farm and property	XY Farm and commerce	YZ Commerce and property	Totals	Percentage
a Politics only	1	3	0	0	0	0	1	5	10
b Politics and profession	5	8	0	1	0	1	0	15	31
c Politics, profession and university	4	4	0	0	1	1	0	10	20
d Politics, profession, university and judicial	4	0	0	0	0	0	0	4	9
e Only judicial (or profession)	3	1	0	1	0	0	1	6	13
f Judicial (or profession) and university	4	0	1	2	1	0	0	8	17
Totals:	21	16	1	4	2	2	2	48	—
%:	48	33	2	8	3	3	3	—	100

2nd period

Occupation and Income	O Professional income	X Farm	Y Commerce and industry	Z Income property	XZ Farm and property	XY Farm and commerce	YZ Commerce and property	Totals	Percentage
a Politics only	1	2	0	0	0	0	1	4	9
b Politics and profession	7	8	0	1	0	2	0	18	40
c Politics, profession and university	4	3	0	1	0	0	0	8	18

TABLE V (Cont.)

		O Professional income	X Farm	Y Commerce and industry	Z Income property	XZ Farm and property	XY Farm and commerce	YZ Commerce and property	Totals	Percentage
d	Politics, profession, university and judicial	0	0	0	0	0	0	0	0	0
e	Only judicial (or profession)	7	1	0	0	0	0	0	8	18
f	Judicial (or profession) and university	5	1	0	1	0	0	0	7	15
	Totals:	24	15	0	3	0	2	1	45	—
	%:	54	33	0	7	0	4	2	—	100

TABLE VI

3rd period

Occupation and Income

		O Professional income	X Farm	Y Commerce and industry	Z Income property	XZ Farm and property	XY Farm and commerce	YZ Commerce and property	Totals	Percentage
a	Politics only	0	0	0	0	0	0	0	0	0
b	Politics and profession	6	1	0	0	0	0	0	7	20
c	Politics, profession and university	3	0	0	0	0	0	0	3	8
d	Politics, profession, university and judicial	0	0	0	0	0	0	0	0	0
3	Only judicial (or profession)	16	0	0	0	0	0	0	16	44

TABLE VI (Cont.)

| | | O | X | Y | Z | XZ | XY | YZ | Totals | Percentage |
		Professional income	Farm	Commerce and industry	Income property	Farm and property	Farm and commerce	Commerce and property		
f	Judicial (or profession) and university	10	0	0	0	0	0	0	10	28
	Totals:	35	1	0	0	0	0	0	36	—
	%:	97	3	0	0	0	0	0	—	100

4th period

Occupation
and
Income

| | | O | X | Y | Z | XZ | XY | YZ | Totals | Percentage |
		Professional income	Farm	Commerce and industry	Income property	Farm and property	Farm and commerce	Commerce and property		
a	Politics only	0	0	0	0	0	0	0	0	0
b	Politics and profession	0	0	0	0	0	0	0	0	0
c	Politics, profession and university	5	0	1	0	1	0	0	7	20
d	Politics, profession, university and judicial	0	0	0	0	0	0	0	0	0
e	Only judicial (or profession)	19	0	0	0	1	0	0	20	54
f	Judicial (or profession) and university	10	0	0	0	0	0	0	10	36
	Totals:	34	0	1	0	2	0	0	37	—
	%:	93	0	2	0	5	0	0	—	100

The first thing one notices in the tables is the high percentage of members of the ruling elite of the Cordobese aristocracy who have as their only source of economic income the results of exercising their profession when they were engaged in the political, judicial, and university sectors. The trend seen through the different periods in this regard is of an increase almost to the exclusion of all the rest; therefore, it would seem, a gradual impoverishment of these ruling elites appears, since it can be supposed that by relying on other economic resources such as lands, business, property, etc., one could count on larger incomes. The percentages of the members of the ruling elites of the Cordobese aristocracy active in the political, judicial, and university sectors who live exclusively from their profession are as follows, distributed by periods:

1924	48%	1951	97%
1937	54%	1960	93%

Even if from the figures given one cannot infer that the Cordobese aristocracy, in general, does not have other sources of income outside their profession, it can, however, be asserted that its ruling elites, in the indicated sectors, do almost exclusively depend upon this source, above all in the third and fourth periods; and that, although to a less degree than in the first and second periods, the percentage is significant of those who have other sources of income besides the exercise of their profession. Among those who had other sources of income, it must be observed that for those who economically abetted themselves from the land—that is, in the primary activity—the trend is for the number to diminish considerably, with a great reduction between the second and third periods. Actually, the percentages are the following:

1924	39%	1951	3%
1937	37%	1960	7%

In the first two periods it would appear that country properties have a significance for the elites of the Cordobese aristocracy, but only for those who participate in the "political" sector. These percentages are influenced greatly by the positions of provincial senator which, in those times, were filled by the estancieros. These facts become evident when compared with those of the ruling elites who were active in the political sector in only the first and second period. We will return to this later.

It is also relevant to see the figures on members of the ruling elites of the Cordobese aristocracy who relied on incomes from industry or commerce. Distributed by periods, they are the following:

1924	8%	1951	0%
1937	3%	1960	0%

A simple statement of the facts enables us to confirm that neither commerce nor industry has been a source of economic income for the ruling elites active in the sectors studied. If there is a small difference between the two first periods and the last two, it can be attributed to the presence of a large number of sons of foreigners recorded in those periods and who were owners of those businesses in Córdoba in that era. The data could also indicate a gradual impoverishment of these ruling elites, although in no case could it be maintained that it was on the basis of these economic sectors (industry and commerce).

Ownership of income property or real estate (at least, economically exploited) would seem also not to have been a source of supplementary income for the ruling elites of the Cordobese aristocracy; at least, that is what the figures indicate, distributed by periods, as follows:

1924	14%	1951	0%
1937	4%	1960	2%

Analysis of the data presented tends to confirm that the principal—and almost basic—source of income for the ruling elites of the Cordobese aristocracy active in the periods analyzed and in the sectors mentioned is the practice of a profession; and if they possessed some other source of income, it existed only in the first periods. It is well to remember that the last two periods are when the ruling elites of the aristocracy were displaced from the political structure of the city; not having other sources of income, they took refuge in the judicial and university sectors, perhaps, even for economic reasons, since their capital is their profession. Therefore, there must have been a political compromise with the governing regimes in these periods for economic reasons. We will analyze this later in more detail.

The problem of the sources of economic power is important not only for determining what role the aristocracy is able to fulfill in the power structure, but also for examining the internal structure of that aristocracy as a social stratum, since the system of social relations is partly maintained by its capacity for expenditure. In our case, and from the data collected, two distinct phases for the Cordobese aristocracy could be established, at least if we look at them through its ruling elites. On the one hand are the first two periods (1924 and 1937) corresponding to the times when the ruling elites of the Cordobese aristocracy participate in the political power structure, and on the other are the two last periods (1951 and 1960) corresponding to the times when the ruling elites of the Cordobese aristocracy did not take part in the political power structure, and retired—almost exclusively—into the judicial and liberal professions and to some extent the university sectors. The first phase, from the point of view of sources of economic power, is characterized by the practice of their profession by the ruling elites with some other economic resources (estancias, property, and commerce or industry); the second phase, from the same point of view, is characterized by the almost exclusive practice of their profession by the ruling elites.

This distinction is important when analyzing the life style and the refinement of social life of the ruling elites of the Cordobese aristocracy; it would seem this way of life could only exist in the first two periods; in the second two, the pursuit of a career and the income derived from it did not permit. The lack of other sources of economic power obliged them to apply themselves to their professions, laying political activity aside.

The general conclusion which can be reached from the data presented is that the ruling elites of the Cordobese aristocracy were never rich, as could be those of Buenos Aires and other Argentine provinces, although at first they could rely on some sources of economic power beyond their professions. With the years, this possibility disappeared, and resulted in an impoverishment of these ruling elites, since they live almost exclusively from their profession. The judiciary, the liberal professions, the University and, in part, politics, can be the areas of activity of the ruling elites of the Cordobese aristocracy. These activities or sources of economic power demand the university diploma, the doctoral parchment. Perhaps the members of the Cordobese aristocracy who rely on other sources of economic power do not form part of its ruling elites or do not represent it as a social stratum and are found incorporated into other social classes (the bourgeois, for example). Some doubt remains with respect to the ruling elites who are active in the political sector, since it would appear that the members of the Cordobese aristocracy who have participated and do participate in the political structure of the city and who rely on other sources of economic power are apt to expand to take part in politics and, according to the facts, in the moments of "institutional crisis" (federal interventions!). But in this respect we do not rely on very impressive facts, yet it is an inference which can be legitimately made, given what happened in the first periods when the Cordobese aristocracy had ruling elites who were active in this institutional sector.

THREE One of the problems which must be explained, with respect to the occupations of the ruling elites of the Cordobese aristocracy, is the degree of professionalism they have, that is, their multi-occupationality, perhaps the consequence of the lack of other sources of economic power. This multi-occupationality, certainly, must be referred to the practice of the professions; therefore, in the tables assembled for this work we have taken the following sectors: political, liberal professions, judicial, and university. This multi-occupationality of the ruling elites of the Cordobese aristocracy is intimately bound to the sources of power and, especially, to the sources of economic power.

Although the result is obvious and the facts make it evident, it is necessary to establish an excluding difference between those participating in the political sector and those in the judicial sector; it concerns activities by their nature (and legally) excludatory. Activity in the university is complementary of both (or can be), whereas activity in the liberal professions excludes activity in the judicial sector. Consequently, those active in the judicial sector can only have complementary activity in the university sector, and those active in the political sector can only have complementary activity in the university and liberal professions areas; or vice versa, those active in liberal professions or in the university can have the political sector as a complementary activity. First we will discuss the members of the ruling elites of the Cordobese aristocracy active in the judicial sector with complementary activity in the university sector. We will leave the second case for later.

The first thing apparent from the tables is the tendency shown by members of the Cordobese aristocracy active in the judicial sector to professionalize themselves, that is, to dedicate themselves increasingly, solely and exclusively, to this professional activity. The data given by periods are quite significant:

1924	13%	1951	44%
1937	18%	1960	54%

This fact carries implicitly a relative tendency for the pursuit of the legal profession to modernize itself, since there is, at least theoretically, a greater dedication and with it a rationalization of its tasks and perhaps a greater effectiveness in performing them. Those who have had political activity and then have dedicated themselves to the law are found only in the first period (9, 0, 0 and 0 percent for the years 1924, 1937, 1951 and 1960, respectively), perhaps as a result of the formation of the first Superior Court of Justice. However, one must dismiss the possibility that positions in the Law, especially those of the upper hierarchy (Superior Court and members of the Supreme Council), were occupational sources for some political members of the ruling elites of the Cordobese aristocracy when they left that area of activity in a particular moment (nevertheless, there are a few cases, and in the first period); consequently, there is no passage from the political to the judicial sector across the ruling elites of the Cordobese aristocracy. Passage in the inverse sense, that is, from the judicial to the political sector is not observed in the periods analyzed, although the phenomenon has occurred—but not often—in the revolutionary periods during which it is customary to resort to the men of justice as a moral reserve without political compromises.

Participation in the university sector by those who are professionally active in the judicial area would appear to have a character complementary to economic income and, perhaps, to actual legal activity or professional prestige. The percentages of joint participation in the judicial and university sectors are quite relevant, and are as follows:

1924	17%	1951	28%
1937	15%	1960	36%

The trend is towards an increase of this multi-occupationality. However, if a correlation among all the members of the judicial is made, at the level dealt with in this work, the proportion tends to decrease slightly, since the percentages are the following:

1924 .... 59%	1951 .... 39%
1937 .... 45%	1960 .... 40%

All these facts tend to show a certain trend towards professionalization of the judicial career for members of the Cordobese aristocracy, although the tendency to multi-occupationality is still very marked. Nevertheless, one will also have to take into account the tendency towards modernization of the University, which will increasingly demand the exclusive dedication of its professors; secondary education also receives many members of the aristocracy who take part in the judicial area, particularly the branch colleges of the National University of Córdoba. It should not be forgotten that a series of courses in secondary education, such as History, Geography, Philosophy, Democratic Education, Spanish, Literature, etc. were given only by lawyers who devoted themselves to the law or the liberal professions. The existence of specialized diplomas will now little by little displace these members of the aristocracy who have this type of multi-occupationality; therefore, they will tend almost obligatorily and for structural reasons to professionalize, that is, to dedicate themselves exclusively to administering justice. Thus, it would seem that judicial activity satisfies the levels of social prestige demanded by the Cordobese aristocracy and offers the opportunity for pursuing its university profession for which it is formally suited. Otherwise, the concentration of the Cordobese aristocracy in this institutional sector would not be understandable.

FOUR With respect to the activity of the ruling elites of the Cordobese aristocracy in the political sector, the data collected show us that it occurred as an exclusive activity only in the first two periods analyzed. This fact, certainly, is closely tied to other variables which we will analyze later, especially referring to ideology and belonging to political parties. The percentages of members of the Cordobese aristocracy who participated in the political sector as their only and exclusive activity, distributed by historical periods, appear as follows:

1924	10%	1951	0%
1937	9%	1960	0%

The ruling elites of the Cordobese aristocracy with exclusive activity in the political field, as seen by our figures, could be found only in the first two periods and principally among the members of those elites having other sources of economic income (land, businesses, properties, etc.); to a certain degree, politics met certain necessities of social or professional prestige; therefore, strictly speaking, they were not professional politicians, since that was not the principal and basic source of their economic income. This is not the *homo politicus* of the Cordobese aristocracy. It would seem that his characteristic is multi-occupationality, that is, participation in the political sector jointly with and superimposed upon participation in the sectors of liberal profession and university. The percentages of double participation—that is, politics and liberal profession—and of triple participation—that is, politics, liberal profession, and University—distributed by historical periods are:

Year	Double participation	Triple participation
1924	31%	20%
1937	40%	18%
1951	20%	8%
1960	0%	20%

The figures given have a certain irregularity and certainly show no trend, although their totals can indeed be significant (1924: 51%, 1937: 58%, 1951: 28%, and 1960: 20%), as it shows

64

a tendency wherein the availability of the professionals of the Cordobese aristocracy is each time less, considered with respect to political offices. In any event, the figures do not appear sufficiently relevant to reach any conclusion. The only thing which can be inferred is that the *homo politicus* of the Cordobese aristocracy must be a professional and, perhaps, from the university; it would seem as if the exercise of a liberal profession and university professorship make the members of the aristocracy available for forming its political ruling elites. But this depends on the ideology and the historic moment; at least this is what one deduces from the data.

The figures of Tables VII and VIII tend to indicate the degree of professionalization and its form among the ruling elites who were active in the political sector of the Cordobese aristocracy.

TABLE VII

1st period Political Professionalization	Up to four years	Between four and ten years	Professionally more than ten years	Not active in politics	Totals	Percentage
a Only at provincial level	7	7	3	1	18	38
b Provincial and national level	0	5	11	0	16	33
c Only at national level	0	0	2	1	3	6
d Not active in politics	1	0	0	10	11	23
Totals:	8	12	16	12	48	—
%:	17	25	33	25	—	100

2nd period

Political Professionalization	Up to four years	Between four and ten years	Professionally more than ten years	Not active in politics	Totals	Percentage
a Only at provincial level	7	6	2	0	15	33
b Provincial and national level	0	4	2	0	6	14
c Only at national level	0	1	9	0	10	22
d Not active in politics	1	0	0	13	14	31
Totals:	8	11	13	13	45	—
%:	15	25	30	30	—	100

TABLE VIII

3rd period Political Professionalization	Up to four years	Between four and ten years	Professionally more than ten years	Not active in politics	Totals	Percentage
a Only at provincial level	8	1	0	0	9	25
b Provincial and national level	0	0	0	0	0	0
c Only at national level	1	2	0	0	3	8
d Not active in politics	0	0	0	24	24	67
Totals:	9	3	0	24	36	—
%:	25	8	0	67	—	100

4th period Political Professionalization	Up to four years	Between four and ten years	Professionally more than ten years	Not active in politics	Totals	Percentage
a Only at provincial level	0	1	0	0	1	3
b Provincial and national level	2	0	1	0	3	8
c Only at national level	3	0	0	0	3	8
d Not active in politics	0	0	0	30	30	81
Totals:	5	1	1	30	37	—
%:	15	3	3	81	—	100

The first thing to be noticed in these tables is that the proportion of members of the Cordobese aristocracy who never were active in politics, although they may have participated in other institutional sectors such as judicial and university, tends ostensibly to increase. The proportions, by periods, are:

1924	.... 23%	1951	.... 67%
1937	.... 31%	1960	.... 81%

And the proportion of those who have been active in politics and who constitute the ruling elites of the Cordobese aristocracy in any sector, also by periods, is the following:

1924	.... 77%	1951	.... 33%
1937	.... 69%	1960	.... 19%

The comparison of these tables reveals the level of political compromise of the ruling elites of the Cordobese aristocracy, since the percentages diminish as they move away from participation in the political sector.

Granted, to characterize the *homo politicus* of the Cordobese aristocracy, one must analyze the degree of professionalism of the ruling elites, that is, the number of years they have been in the political power structure, and the level of this activity, whether it has been on a provincial or national level or both, almost as a political career. The members of the political ruling elites of the Cordobese aristocracy who were active in that sector for more than ten years, to a certain degree, constitute the *homo politicus*. The percentages by periods are the following:

1924	33%	1951	0%
1937	30%	1960	3%

Heeding the figures given and on the basis of the definition given (activity in the area for more than ten years), the *homo politicus* of the Cordobese aristocracy appeared in only the first two periods analyzed in this study, that is, between 1918 and 1943, since, later, political leaders from the Cordobese aristocracy appear only in an incidental fashion. And the proportion of the members of the Cordobese aristocracy who appeared in the political sector in an incidental fashion appears as more or less constant and without any trend. The percentages of this incidental participation in the political sector by members of the Cordobese aristocracy, distributed by historical periods, are:

1924	17%	1951	25%
1937	17%	1960	13%

The figures show a certain occasional availability for political activity by members of the Cordobese aristocracy, regardless of the ruling ideology. The increase in the Peronista period is significant for pointing up the availability of the Cordobese aristocracy for access to political power. These individuals were active in politics less than four years and in general occupied only one position and without continuing. With an intermediate participation, that is, more than four and less than ten years, the percentages are the following:

1924	.... 25%	1951	.... 8%
1937	.... 25%	1960	.... 3%

This table and these percentages tend to resemble those of persons who have served in a professional manner in the political sector, meaning that, save for the incidental participation of the members of the Cordobese aristocracy in the political sector—which remains more or less constant in all the periods—the *homo politicus* of the Cordobese aristocracy only existed in the first two periods analyzed, when its ruling elites participated in the political power structure. And, once again, we comprehend an ideological statement which we will analyze later.

The distribution of political activity by sphere of activity of the ruling elites of the Cordobese aristocracy, that is, those who participated at the national or provincial level or both, aside from the clear distinction between the first two and the last two periods, shows us nothing relevant. But it would seem that the incarnation of the *homo politicus* exists in those who were active either at the national level or at the national provincial levels; the one who was active only at the provincial level does not tend to represent the *homo politicus* of the Cordobese aristocracy, since the former were the only ones who were almost entirely university professionals living from their liberal profession, from the university chair, and from the political activity which were characteristics of this *homo politicus* of the Cordobese aristocracy. It concerns the idea of the old doctoral aristocracy before 1918. However, some differences appear between the *homo politicus* of the first and second epochs, tending, logically, to represent politics prior to 1918. These differences are: a) the members of the political ruling elites of the first epoch, concurrently

with exercising a profession, served in the University, while
those found in the second period pursued only liberal
professions; b) the members of the political ruling elites of the
first period were wont to have another source of economic
income—above all, those who were active at the national
level, exclusively—while those of the second epoch lived only
from their profession, as an activity parallel to the political
function. It must also be stated that the data we have for the
third and fourth periods do not permit us to define the *homo
politicus* of this epoch, since his activity was always incidental
and never professional.

VI

Aristocratic
Ideology

ONE Nothing new is said if one maintains that ideology, to a great extent, can define the social strata, and very especially when dealing with social strata such as an aristocracy. Since it constitutes a social stratum belonging to a social stratification system which appears as residual in the face of the process of development, it normally has a conservative ideology, since it defends the established order and rests on tradition. Nevertheless, historically it has not always appeared thus. At present, certainly, we are not going to go into the theoretical problems of ideologies, and even less into the sticky problems of the correlations between social strata and ideology.

From the data we have and the insinuations arising out of the information already analyzed in this volume, we will define the ideology of the Cordobese aristocracy by two variables: belonging to political parties, and the liberal or Catholic position within them. We are perfectly aware of all the limitations imposed by this definition; nonetheless, we believe, they have genuine grounds in the subject we are studying. And since our intent is to describe a trend and not define a stratum, we believe our statement can be valid. Therefore, obviously, we will limit our conclusions to the social stratum we are analyzing in the present work.

On several occasions throughout this volume, we have seen the necessity for solving this problem of the ideology of the ruling elites of the Cordobese aristocracy, due to the very marked break it shows between the ruling elites of the first and second periods and the ruling elites of the third and fourth periods; one could say that it has produced, historically, a break in the participation of the ruling elites of the Cordobese aristocracy in the power structure of the city, and especially, of the political ruling elites. The social function of these ruling elites has changed in the power structure of the community, and, therefore, it is quite possible that their own internal structure and the representivity they have are altered.

Before presenting the tables with the data obtained, some clarifications and definitions must be made with respect to the variables used. As regards belonging to political parties, it must be pointed out that only political parties which we can define as basic were taken into consideration, that is, those which have been the root of the new political parties arising since 1955. Therefore, for example, within the Democratic Party, in the last period, we have included the Christian Democrats, the Independent Civic Party, the UDELPA, and the Popular Conservative Party. The reason for this inclusion, certainly, is not arbitrary since, on one hand, the people who have joined these new parties come from the Democratic Party (they or their fathers), and on the other, the people joining these new parties did not participate in (or did so rarely) the power structure of Córdoba. Within the Radical Party is included the People's Radical Civic Union as well as the UCRI. It must not be forgotten that, from the point of view of its leaders, the latter is a separation from the former. Nor must one forget that the UCRI was the government power in 1960. And within the Socialist and Peronista Parties are included all the party and ideological divisions and subdivisions which were later produced.

It must also be pointed out that, in the analysis we will make, we have excluded from our sample those who did and do participate in the judicial sector, without belonging to political parties. The reasons appear obvious, and we have included such persons with the independents group. With respect to the liberal or Catholic position, we have considered those who took part in the judicial sector, since it does not carry with it a political compromise which the Judicial Power, at least formally, cannot demonstrate. It must be added also that the political vicissitudes which have run through the city could have compromised many magistrates without implying a belonging to political parties; this fact has especial importance in the third period we analyze. And, finally, belonging to political parties by the members of the judicial is of no interest, since they cannot form ruling elites in the Cordobese aristocracy.

One point, perhaps more delicate, is that referring to the second variable by which we analyze the ideology of the ruling elites of the Cordobese aristocracy: the liberal or Catholic position. This distinction arose from the data we possessed; nevertheless, it has been a very decisive variable in defining the ideology of the ruling elites which the key informants of the present investigation gave. It would seem that the Cordobese aristocracy has always had liberal ruling elites and Catholic ruling elites, with a right and a left wing. We do not know if the designation we use is the most correct, but the data brought it out. In any event, it is convenient to mention that when one speaks of liberal ruling elites one refers only to a broader position with respect to other democratic ideologies and with respect to the orthodox Catholic thought; and when one speaks of Catholic ruling elites one refers only to a position of ostensible Catholic militancy that is narrower with respect to other democratic ideologies. The liberal ruling elites were more secular, although not anti-Catholic, while the Catholic ruling elites were very orthodox in Catholic thought. Further, it must be stated that this variable affects all the political parties, except perhaps the Socialist Party, which is radically liberal in our terminology. Nevertheless, this variable is going to be changing with the passage of time and therefore affecting the internal structure of these same ruling elites of the Cordobese aristocracy.

We believe that these explanations, even though short, are no less important; we must recognize that they have been of great help in understanding much of our subject of study, above all in understanding the break between the first and last two periods and in understanding the changes of the ruling elites of the Cordobese aristocracy and their presence in the power structure of Córdoba through all the years, although with a declining trend; they are what enabled us to understand the availability of the ruling elites of the Cordobese aristocracy and their marginality in the power structure of the city.

TWO In what follows, we will analyze the ruling elites of the Cordobese aristocracy by means of two variables: belonging to political parties, and liberal or Catholic position. The figures obtained, distributed by historical periods and on the basis of these variables, are presented in Table IX.

The first thing one notices in the figures is the enormous percentage of members of the ruling elites of the Cordobese aristocracy who belonged to the Democratic Party in the first two historical periods analyzed, completely disappearing in the third period, to show a resurgence—for causes we will analyze later—in the last period. The percentages, distributed by historical periods, are:

1924:	83%	1951:	0%
1937:	82%	1960:	54%

If one compares this table and these percentages with the members of the ruling elites of the Cordobese aristocracy who belonged to the Radical Party, the figures become more significant:

74

TABLE IX

		1st period			2nd period			3rd period			4th period		
		Lib. Y	Cath. Z	Total	Lib. Y	Cath. Z	Total	Lib. Y	Cath. Z	Total	Lib. Y	Cath. Z	Total
a	Democratic	24	5	29	17	10	27	0	0	0	2	5	7
b	Radical	1	5	6	3	3	6	0	2	2	1	4	5
c	Socialist	0	0	0	0	0	0	0	0	0	1	0	1
d	Peronista	0	0	0	0	0	0	3	12	15	0	0	0
e	Independent	8	5	13	7	5	12	3	16	19	6	18	24
	Totals:	33	15	48	27	18	45	6	30	36	10	27	37
	%:	69	31	100	60	40	100	17	83	100	27	73	100

| 1924: | 17% | 1951: | 30% |
| 1937: | 18% | 1960: | 40% (With the UCRI) |

The tables clearly show us that the ruling elites of the Cordobese aristocracy were members of the Democratic Party in the first two periods and that, only rarely, did the Cordobese aristocracy have elites in the Radical Party. This is clear. What happened in the other historical periods is something quite different. It must be remembered that in 1924 the Democratic Party was the governing party in the Province and of the opposition in the Nation; and in 1937 the Democratic Party was the opposition in the Province and in power in the Nation. In the third period, the Democratic Party is absent from the power structure. In the fourth, it appears in a very relative fashion, through other parties springing from it. The Radical Party has always been in the power structure, either as a governing power in 1937 and 1960 (the UCRI), or as the opposition in 1924 and 1951.

The increase in members of the Cordobese aristocracy who belong to the Radical Party, in the third period, is perhaps due to the fact that it was the only "real" party in opposition to Peronismo; so the increase in the fourth period is perhaps due to the fact that the separation from the Radical Party which the UCRI signified could very well represent the Cordobese aristocracy. However, what seems apparent is that after the third period the Democratic Party no longer numbers ruling elites representing the Cordobese aristocracy, or else that the Cordobese aristocracy has changed in such a way that the ruling elites of the Democratic Party have broken away from it. The Democratic Party ceases to represent the ideology of the ruling elites of the Cordobese aristocracy who participate in the power of the city after the third period; and "new" ruling elites coming from the aristocracy are formed which are those who take part in the power. Here one sees very clearly the differences between the residual ruling elites (those of the Democratic Party who do not participate in the power) and the emerging ruling elites (those of other parties who participate in the power); the first are traditional (those prior to the third period) and the second are availables (those coming after the third period).

What appears to be significant, perhaps to demonstrate how the Democratic Party no longer represents the ideology of the ruling elites of the Cordobese aristocracy after the third period, are the figures of the third period in which it is seen that 88 percent of the members figuring in the power from the Cordobese aristocracy are with Peronismo, and only 12 percent are with the Radical Party; the last period shows a high percentage of members of the aristocracy in the power structure, but it is owing to their being with the UCRI, which not only absorbed Peronismo (?) but established a conservative (?) ideology.

The most general conclusion to be drawn from the data given is that the Cordobese aristocracy creates ruling elites in the political parties having access to the power structure; when the parties cease to have a chance for access to power, new ruling elites are formed among the parties which have this chance. It would seem that the aristocracies need, inexorably, the power structure; that they do not resist the marginality of power. Granted, the ruling elites of the Cordobese aristocracy who can no longer take part in the power structure become *traditional ruling elites,* and the ruling elites who can participate in the power structure become the *available ruling elites;* but this entails implicitly a spreading out of the aristocracy as a social stratum. The place left by the former will be occupied by new ruling elites belonging to other emerging social strata.

The variable inserted here, to explain this circulation of the ruling elites, is the process of industrial development of the City of Córdoba, since with its initiation begins this "spreading out" among the ruling elites of the power aristocracy; faced with industrialization, the ruling elites remain: some as emerging (those who come with the process of industrial development) and others as residuals, who spread out in their turn among those who remain as availables and, therefore, spur the process and those who remain as traditional and, therefore, resist the process. This is clearly seen in the adherence of ruling elites to the Democratic Party. When the process of industrialization did not exist, the ruling elites of the Cordobese aristocracy identified themselves with the Democratic Party, which participated in the power structure of Córdoba during the first two periods; then the ruling elites of the Cordobese aristocracy, faced with the beginning of the process of industrial development, with new emerging elites linked to this process, branched into the traditionals who no longer take part in the power because they are nostalgic for the situation prior to the process of industrial development (they identify with the Democratic Party, as before) and into the availables, who can take part in the power structure because they value the process of industrial development—they identify with the Peronista Party, primarily, and with the "Desarrollismos" (UCRI, UDELPA, Christian Democrats, Popular Conservatives, etc.). Important to know here is which part of the Cordobese aristocracy has traditional ruling elites and which part has available ruling elites. We will analyze this later.

This branching out of the ruling elites of the Cordobese aristocracy after the third period cannot be separated from the process followed by the ruling elites of the Cordobese aristocracy which we analyzed in the previous pages, particularly with reference to their impoverishment due to the lack of other sources of economic power and with regard to their professional tradition. The traditional ruling elites—that is, those who participate neither in the political power nor the process of industrialization, owing to the previously mentioned characteristics—will tend relatively to concentrate in the independent profession and the university sectors, while the available ruling elites will tend to concentrate in the sectors of politics, judicial, university, and independent profession, but tied to the process of industrialization. Nevertheless, the problem always remains of the ruling elites who are attuned to the old ideology of the first two periods, and those who respond to the new ideology of the last two periods; that is, those who relate to the preindustrial community and those who react to the industrial community, because this fact explains the circulation of the ruling elites of the Cordobese aristocracy.

THREE The distinction of the ruling elites of the Cordobese aristocracy between liberals and Catholics, at the margin of the political party they represent, gives us the following percentages, by historical periods:

1924:	liberals: 69%	1951:	liberals: 17%
	Catholics: 31%		Catholics: 83%
1937:	liberals: 60%	1960:	liberals: 27%
	Catholics: 40%		Catholics: 73%

The first thing one notices clearly is that, as the years pass, there is a decrease of the liberal ruling elites and an increase in the Catholic ruling elites of the Cordobese aristocracy in the power structure. Within the Cordobese aristocracy, the liberal ruling elites tend to appear as residual and the Catholic ruling elites as emerging; the former represent the Cordobese aristocracy more in the first two periods and the latter in the last two periods. Thus could be explained, in general, which ruling elites remain as traditionals and which as availables, that is, those who move away from political power and the industrialization process, and those who move into political power (in the new parties) and the industrialization process, allying themselves with the sectors emerging from this process. These figures become more significant when one sees the high percentage of representatives of the Catholic sector in the Judicial Power, as they are incorporated in the political party sector as independents. The high percentage of Catholics in the third period is tied to affiliation with Peronismo in the power structure; the liberals, is seems, did not compromise themselves to Peronismo.

Distinguishing the ruling elites of the Cordobese aristocracy between those of the first and those of the last periods, it would seem that the ruling elites of the Cordobese aristocracy who were liberal became Catholic, at least among those who took part in the power of Córdoba. Therefore, the Catholic character is what makes the ruling elites of the Cordobese aristocracy remain available for access to power, since it is they who incorporate into the industrialization process of Córdoba. And here, it is convenient to recall some other general characteristics of the Cordobese aristocracy, particularly those tied to family tradition, such as connection with the commercial and industrial sectors, closeness regarding the sons of foreigners, and, above all, closeness in the face of persons who came from sectors of a lower social level. Finally, the "Catholic" ruling elites are the ones who join with the new commercial and industrial sectors emerging from the process of industrial development; they share with them functions in the city power structure and incorporate these people into the Cordobese aristocracy through marriage (with the corresponding university diploma, of course). The Cordobese aristocracy, therefore, and seen through the analysis made of the ruling elites representing it, changes its internal structure to the point where perhaps it ceases to be an aristocracy; nevertheless, one can continue speaking of it, since it sustains marriage as the institutionalized channel of access to the aristocracy, preceded by the rite of passage of the university diploma, and exercise of the university profession as its basic and fundamental occupation, and through which it takes part in the economic system of the city. The existence of the moral and religious values is obvious, other things being equal. But what remains of the doctoral aristocracy?

FOUR The ruling elites of the Cordobese aristocracy are distinguished between those of the first two and those of the last two historical periods by belonging to political parties and by their liberal and Catholic position when they took part in the power structure of Córdoba. A trend of the ruling elites of the aristocracy (impoverishment, professionalization, etc.) conditions the passage of primacy from one type of elite to another type of elite: from the traditionals to the availables. We now would like to introduce a new variable which, to a certain extent, tends to explain this passage from primacy of one type of aristocratic elite to another. This variable is the "club life" or the clubman as an element of the ruling elites, especially of the political ruling elites.

The data given in Table X clearly show, on the one hand, the obvious correlation existing between clubman and belonging to the Democratic Party, in the first two periods, by the political elites of the Cordobese aristocracy and, on the other, the lack of correlation between clubman and belonging to political parties (whatever they might be) in the last two periods. Thus we have it that 84% and 80% of the men of the political elites active in the first two periods were members of the Democratic Party; in the other periods it is so insignificant that it is not worth pursuing. On the other hand, one notices, in the data shown, that the condition of clubman was not a characteristic of the political elites of the Cordobese aristocracy who belonged to the Radical Party. By clubs we mean those exclusively social, omitting sports and culture.

From the data shown, it would seem that the club life was, in the first two periods, a condition for the political elites of the Cordobese aristocracy, especially when it referred to

TABLE X

Club and politics	1st period			2nd period			3rd period			4th period		
	Dem.	Rad.	Ind.	Dem.	Rad.	Ind.	Dem.	Rad.	Ind.	Dem.	Rad.	Ind.
	X	Y	Z	X	Y	Z	X	Y	Z	X	Y	Z
Clubman and politician	21	0	0	16	1	0	30	4	2	7	7	23
Clubman and not politician	5	0	4	1	0	3	0	0	0	0	0	0
Not clubman and politician	4	5	0	6	4	0	1	1	0	2	0	0
Not clubman and not politician	0	1	8	3	1	10	4	1	1	1	3	1
Totals:	30	6	12	26	6	13	35	2	1	4	4	22

Editor's Note: The totals shown for the third and fourth periods differ markedly from the totals obtained by arithmetical check of the individual entries. The entire textual discussion of "club and politics" is obviously not based on the data actually given in Table X.

belonging to the Democratic Party; it would seem that the political elites of the Cordobese aristocracy who belonged to the Democratic Party were made in the Club. Nonetheless, the introduction of the liberal and Catholic variable permits us to draw some conclusions, since the condition of clubman is identified with the liberal political elites and not with the Catholics of the Cordobese aristocracy. Perhaps on this account the disappearance of these liberal elites from the power structure coincides with the disappearance from the club life of the new Catholic political elites who do participate in the city power structure—now not as members of the Democratic Party, although they had always participated in an incidental manner, as we already have seen. Thus, it would seem that the club life has somewhat influenced the liberal political elites of the Cordobese aristocracy and their destiny in the power structure. Therefore, we believe that these facts would require greater refinement, which we cannot make through lack of more conclusive data.

Nevertheless, one could conclude, although only as an hypothesis, that the club life is tied to the liberal political elites, since it would seem that the Club has ceased to constitute the manner of becoming a politician and of forming the political elites of the Cordobese aristocracy, as would appear was the case in the first two periods studied. And the club life has many characteristics which, in some way, must define those liberal political elites, but, above all, which must have decided their destiny in the power structure of Córdoba.

VII

Traditional Elites and Available Elites

ONE We now intend to state the problem of the "destiny" of the Cordobese aristocracy, in the four historical periods studied, through the functions performed by its ruling elites in the community power structure. We understand that changes in these functions reflect the process of Cordobese industrial development. These changes in the functions of the ruling elites in the power structure of the community have altered the internal structure of the social stratum involved—the aristocracy; nevertheless, this social stratum could maintain itself in the power structure, thanks to certain of its characteristics, but basically because it was a doctoral aristocracy.

Therefore, we will begin our study with a characterization of the Cordobese aristocracy before 1918, that is, when its ruling elites constituted a *power elite,* because they controlled all the power and because they exercised it in a manner prescribed by the social stratum. After 1918, institutionalized mechanisms are created for the exchange or circulation of the ruling elites in the community power structure; and, therefore, the ruling elites of the Cordobese aristocracy begin, in a small degree, to share control of the power structure, since the new ruling elites begin to appear together with the new social sectors which are emerging from the process of community development (immigration; complexity of the economy; appearance of an incipient bourgeois, commercial first and industrial and financial later; functional necessities of the State, etc. etc.).

The first two periods analyzed, although they show a tendency for the ruling elites of the Cordobese aristocracy to lose influence in decisions taken in the community, to a certain extent "represent" that social stratum in the city power structure. From 1943, it would seem that the matter changes, although the trend continues that the ruling elites of the Cordobese aristocracy tend to lessen their participation in the power structure and to concentrate in certain institutional sectors (judicial, university, and independent professions). But also, the ruling elites have changed, since from being democrats and liberals in the first two periods, they have become desarollistas and Catholics in the last two periods; the first constituting the *traditional ruling elites,* and the second, the *available ruling elites.* This distinction can explain, on the one hand, the eclipse of the ruling elites of the Cordobese aristocracy and, on the other, their permanency in the Cordobese power structure.

The criterion which distinguishes these ruling elites of the Cordobese aristocracy is their position in the face of the process of industrial development of the City, since the traditionals tend to draw away from the process and, therefore, to resist it, because they represent the preindustrial society in which the aristocracy is the highest stratum of the estate system of social stratification; whereas the availables tend to incorporate themselves into the process and, therefore, to encourage it by an alliance with those who represent the industrial society in which the bourgeois is the highest stratum of the class system of social stratification. And thus, the ruling elites who represent the aristocracy as a social stratum of an estate system of social stratification tend to eclipse, and the ruling elites who represent the aristocracy as the upper class of a class system of social stratification tend to stay in the power structure. The decisive factor of this distinction is the infrastructure of the industrial development which changes the ideology of the Cordobese aristocracy: those who resist the social change of the process are the democrats and liberals and those who encourage the social change of the process are the desarollistas (whatever the party) and Catholics.

This double function of the ruling elites of the Cordobese aristocracy in the face of the process of Cordobese industrial development determines the destiny of the aristocracy as a social stratum; the *traditional elites* relegate it to a residual condition since they place it in a system of social stratification which tends to disappear through the pressure of the process of industrial development; the *available elites* place it in an emerging condition since they incorporate it into a system of social stratification which tends to impose itself through the pressure of the process of industrial development of Córdoba, as long as this remains constant and progressive; the *traditional elites* carry it to the eclipse of the Cordobese aristocracy and the *available elites* bring it to the formation of the incipient bourgeois. The new classes, for their accession to power, inexorably need the old available social strata.

TWO Throughout all that has been said, however, there always remains suspended the explanation of the problem of how the Cordobese aristocracy, in spite of the loss of functions in the Cordobese power structure, can have available ruling elites for access to it, although these ruling elites no longer represent the Cordobese aristocracy as a social stratum, but rather the new sector emerging from the process of industrial development; finally, why can members of the Cordobese aristocracy be ruling elites of other social sectors? why are they available? why do they remain in the power structure of Córdoba?

The answers to these questions can only be found in the structural characteristics of this Cordobese aristocracy. In the first place, we have seen that access to the Cordobese aristocracy, before 1918 and later, in the periods analyzed in this work, and on the basis of the ruling elites, was achieved only through the institutionalized route of matrimony. Foreigners as well as sons of foreigners, persons coming from commercial or industrial sectors as well as persons from lower sectors, Cordobese as well as those from other provinces, whenever they satisfied definite requirements, had access to marriage with a member of the Cordobese aristocracy; and, therefore, incorporation into that social stratum. The basic requirement for marriage was the university diploma, the professional career. Matrimony and the university diploma make clear, on the one hand, that a stratum of the estate type is involved and, on the other, that access to this estate is through acquired and not appointed characteristics of the social person. This fact permits it to continue as a social stratum because it shows a great "porosity" for accepting new members and, therefore, not an excessive rigidity. The constant and regulated renewal of its members maintains the strength of the social stratum in the community structure.

In the second place, we have seen that the sources of economic power of the Cordobese aristocracy, at least in the periods analyzed, were based more on professional pursuit than on other economic sources such as lands, business, industry, or property; therefore, an aristocracy is involved which, in general, has always been poor and which through the years shows a tendency to subsist economically more and more through professional activity. This characteristic gives it a great "flexibility" to adjust itself to new situations, such as the process of Cordobese industrial development, and therefore, to possess availables who form ruling elites covering other social and economic sectors. These availables offer their professional services in the areas of politics, the university, the liberal professions, and the law. These characteristics of flexibility and adaptation have been clearly verified in the investigation which served as the basis for this volume.

In the third place, we have seen that the ideology of the ruling elites of the Cordobese aristocracy at no time has been singular and consolidated but, to the contrary, has been dual and flexible (accommodating, in the good sense of the word). With the crisis of belonging to the Democratic Party and from the liberal position, new ruling elites appear who belong to desarrollista parties and with a Catholic position which places them at the head of the fights of partisan factions (desarrollismo and Catholicism). This characteristic gives the aristocracy the capacity always to have available new ruling elites, especially in the political field of the community power structure. The Cordobese aristocracy has the capacity to delegate its ruling elites to take part in the power, because it has always had a dual ideology and has not been tied to one political party; circumstances determine the superiority of some or of others. Among the circumstances it is useful to point out the revolutionary periods (1930-32, 1943-46, 1955-58, and 1966-?), which regularly have interrupted the country's institutional development. At these times there has always been assistance from the ruling elites of the Cordobese aristocracy or, perhaps, these periods have always produced ruling elites from the Cordobese aristocracy, precisely because of the porosity, flexibility, and availability of this social stratum; in 1955, and perhaps in 1930, the *traditional elites* of the Cordobese aristocracy were in power and in 1943 and 1966—perhaps, in part, in 1930—the *available elites* were in power! The Federal interventions—of which Córdoba had many—also favored this presence of the Cordobese aristocracy in the power structure.

These characteristics of the ruling elites of the Cordobese aristocracy clearly point out how this aristocracy tends to disappear as a social stratum (it is a question of a residual social stratum in a new system of social stratification: the class system!), but it will always have available people who form ruling elites capable of representing the new social sectors which emerge from the process of industrial development because they are, essentially, doctorales, that is, because they are university professionals ready to offer their services—inexorably necessary—to the new sectors and to the new needs of the process of industrial development; the fact that they never have had a great economic capacity and that they are very open to receive new members belonging to other social sectors makes them capable of incorporating into the new social classes which emerge from the process of industrial development of the City of Córdoba. But it carries implicitly the *eclipse of an aristocracy* as a social stratum and the availability of its members for access to power by representing the new social sectors; the liberals will incorporate into the new semiprofessional classes, and the Catholics into the new industrial and financial bourgeois. But this incorporation does not mean appearing as an accomplished fact, but as sharing in the establishment of these social classes, to be basic elements of the new social classes emerging from the process of industrial development by virtue of their doctoral or professional character. This is the misery and the grandeur of the Cordobese aristocracy in its participation in the power structure of the city in the last fifty years. The destiny of the Cordobese aristocracy has depended upon the circulation of its ruling elites as the traditionals *descend* to the semiprofessional classes and the availables *remain* in the new industrial and financial bourgeoisie. The institutional sectors which gain influence in community decisions, such as business and finance, labor, and mass communications media, will turn to the Cordobese aristocracy to represent them in the power structure; the institutional sectors permanent in their influence on decisions taken in the community (Church, Military, and Government) will turn to the *available ruling elites* (desarrollistas and Catholics) to represent them in the power structure. These structural elements, emerging from the process of industrial development, set the circulation of the ruling elites of the Cordobese aristocracy into motion, in that they *retain* those who encourage the industrial development process, and *edge out* those who resist it, that is, they lower them to the semiprofessional classes. The process of industrial development determines the ruling elites who participate in the power structure of the City of Córdoba; and among these ruling elites are found, and will continue to be found, members of the old Cordobese aristocracy, because they are doctorales.

APPENDIX I

Power Structure and Power Elite in an Urban Community*

ONE The present work constitutes an analysis of the empirical data obtained in an investigation carried out in the city of Córdoba between 1963/65, on the basis of a pattern of investigation already applied in two cities in the United States and one in England.[1] The objective of the investigation was of a comparative nature; therefore, the four cities studied had a series of common variables,[2] and certainly also a set of dissimilar variables.[3] In the study, special emphasis was placed precisely on the differential variables possessed by Córdoba with respect to the other American and British cities.

From the data obtained it was deduced, however, that two variables, intimately related to each other, played a decisive role in the structuring of power in Córdoba: a) the recent process of industrialization of Córdoba, and b) the connection of the social structure of Córdoba in a global society which is found in a determined state of development.

* Published in *Aportes* (Paris: No. 2, October 1966), pp. 80-105. The present work is based on an investigation carried out jointly with Professor Delbert C. Miller and Eva Chamorro Greca; therefore, the data used in this work belong to that investigation, and many of the conclusions, as well as some interpretations presented in this book, to a great extent belong to the authors of that investigation. A comparison of this work with that investigation will reveal the "original" in this volume.

These two variables, certainly, were not found in the other cities studied under the same pattern of investigation. Finally, it was a question of the incidence of the process of economic development, begun via industrialization, in the community power structure.

In the functioning of this process, the empirical data showed that the different elements of the power structure of Córdoba appeared as residual and emerging elements; that is, there appeared elements of the power structure belonging to a social structure of traditional type and elements of the power structure belonging to a social structure of modern type,[4] to use a symbol very much in vogue at the moment, in a contiguous and superimposed form; in turn, permanent elements of the power structure appeared, but with different functions. These substantiations, finally, serve to define a fixed *stadium* of development with regard to the power structure, which can be called "in transition."[5]

The residual as well as the emerging elements are defined in this context as function of the dynamics of the economic development (in our case, of the industrial development), since they tend, respectively, to resist or encourage the process; therefore, these expressions do not carry any evaluative weight, but are simply functional to a dynamics which appears empirically.

The dynamics of the industrialization process were slowly and gradually affecting all the social structures of Córdoba.[6] The power structure, certainly, had not been able to remain apart from this impact; therefore, exactly, it is found in a definite stadium or state of structuration, which can be designated transitional; but also—and this is fundamental—it appears to us as a decided trend of the structural development of power that it tends to acquire a definite form, although (as always happens) perhaps it never attains realization as a complete whole.[7] That state and that trend of the development of the power structure of Córdoba are the bases which permit us to show the components of the power structure as residual elements and as emerging elements. And this means only that the power structure of Córdoba is at present slowly and gradually undergoing a process of adjustment or adaptation to the functional demands of the industrialization process as it spreads and imposes itself in all dimensions of the social structure of the community.

The data collected in the city of Córdoba with respect to the power structure point out in eloquent form: a) that the power structure, at present, is a result of the process of industrialization; b) that this result of the process of industrialization is found in a definite state of transition; c) that this state of transition is noticed by the contiguous and superimposed presence of residual components and emerging components in the power structure of Córdoba; d) that those residual and emerging components of the power structure show a tendency to structure themselves in a definite form as a whole.

TWO In order to avoid misunderstandings, it would be useful here to give some explanations: the first—and perhaps most obvious—is that the studies on the power structure of a community must never be confused with the studies of the power structure of global societies, because it is concerned with vastly different matters; nor can generalizations of various studies on the power structure of different communities (especially urban) represent the power structure of a global society; the second—and perhaps more simple—is that in the present study it is taken for granted that Córdoba is found affected by a process of industrialization; therefore, it will not be attempted to demonstrate or explain this fact, but only as it affects the power structure;[8] the third—and perhaps the most debatable—is that the present study is not about power elites (of the type of C. Wright Mills, for example[9]), but about the structure of the power; therefore, it is not tied to fixed social classes or to the social stratification or to those who rule;[10] nevertheless, and with attention to the necessity of confronting this subject, we will insinuate a series of hypotheses on the problem of the power elites with respect to the data obtained in the study on the power structure—hypotheses which, necessarily, must be empirically verified in order to have validity.

   THREE The empirical investigation departed from a theory of "the interrelated components of power of the community" which William Form and Delbert C. Miller had developed and applied in other similar investigations.[11] According to this theory, the power structure of a community is created through an interrelation of components which mutually condition one another. These components were:

   a) The institutional power structure of the global society, which refers to the relative distribution of power among the social or global institutions;

   b) The institutionalized power structure of the community, which refers to the relative distribution of power among the community or local institutions;

   c) The power complex of the community, which consists of the arrangement of power among the permanent or temporary organizations, the associations of special interests, and the informal groups which appear when matters or projects of interest to the community are planned;

   d) The top influentials of the community, which refers to those persons considered as having great influence and power in getting things of interest to the community accomplished; and

   e) The key influentials of the community, which refers to those persons whom the top influentials consider as their leaders for getting things done.

   Each one of these components of the power structure, according to this theory, must influence what happens and, in its entirety, must constitute the community power structure; that is, must be the source of formation and perfection of the decisions which interest the community in any of its sectors.[12]

The fields of interest of the community, in the study, where the decisions are applied, are thirteen institutional sectors: government, military, religion, education, political parties, business and finance, labor, independent professions, mass communications, society and wealth, culture and art, social welfare, and entertainment or recreation. In this way, it was attempted to trace, in general outline, the most representative institutional sectors where decisions are taken which interest the community as a whole. These areas, in each one of the components of the power structure, have a relative distribution of influence to succeed in accomplishing things when a problem or matter of community interest arises. Therefore, each institutional sector must condition the power structure and arrange or integrate the different components of the community power structure.

It is not attempted here to trace the methodological problem nor the techniques which were applied to obtain the relative distribution of power in these institutional sectors and of the selection of these institutional sectors which appeared in the community which is the object of our study; the interested reader can satisfy his curiosity from the book *De la industria al poder* by the authors of the investigation,[13] and in the works published in *The Administrative Science Quarterly* and in *The American Journal of Sociology* by the same authors.[14] Nevertheless, it is fitting to point out that the perspective of the present analysis is comparative; that is, it is made on the basis of the common and differential characteristics of the four cities studied using the same pattern of investigation.

FOUR The arrangement of the empirical data collected with respect to each one of the components of the power structure of Córdoba, presented in simple terms, was as follows:

1. The institutional power structure of the global society arranged the various sectors as follows, according to: a)

relative strength; b) influence in getting things done when a problem of community interest arises; and c) influence in the nation when projects or matters of national interest are discussed:

1. Military sector
2. Religion sector
3. Business and finance sector
4. Government sector
5. Labor sector
6. Society and wealth sector
7. Political parties sector
8. Liberal professions sector
9. Education sector
10. Mass communications sector
11. Social welfare sector
12. Culture and art sector
13. Entertainment or recreation sector

As is discovered from this distribution and arrangement of the sectors by their relative weight in getting things done when a project or matter of interest to society arises, based on the criterion of the judges (and which was controlled by a series of "panels" of experts)[15], the most influential sectors are: military, religion, business and finance, government, labor, and society and wealth.

2. The institutionalized power structure of the local community distributed the various sectors, under the same criteria, in the following order:

1. Religion sector
2. Business and finance sector
3. Government sector
4. Labor sector
5. Military sector
6. Mass communications sector
7. Education sector
8. Political parties sector
9. Society and wealth sector
10. Independent professions sector

11. Culture and art sector
12. Social welfare sector
13. Entertainment or recreation sector

As is seen from this distribution and arrangement of the sectors by their relative weight in getting things done when a project or matter of interest for the local community arises, the most influential areas are: religion, business and finance, government, labor, military, and mass communications media.

The first thing one notices when comparing these arrangements of the sectors at a national and local level is that the same five sectors are considered as the most influential for getting things done, although they are ordered in a different way. In this ordination, the most notable is the passage of the military sector from first place at the national level to fifth place at the local level. The comparative analysis of these data shows the existence of a high degree of correlation among the sectors of greater influence of the national and local orders: the same occurs with the sectors of less influence. This high degree of correlation among the sectors most influential in decisions points out the conditioning of local decisions by national decisions when matters of interest to those sectors are concerned.

3. The power complex of Córdoba—that is, the organisms or associations which have influence in getting things done in the community—was principally made up of the following:

A political party
A business organization
Two company associations
Two newspapers
A Catholic organization
The regional labor confederation
The University authorities (as Council)

As is inferred from these data, the elements of the power complex of Córdoba belonging to the business and finance, mass communications, and political parties sectors are more important than what is inferred from the institutionalized power structure; and, to the contrary, the military and religion sectors were less important than the former. It is clear that for these sectors, as well as for the government sector, it is very difficult to rely on associations beyond their bureaucratic structure. This does not occur in the religion sector, which can have many opportunities; therefore, it is understood that it has less influence in this component of the power structure. Interesting to note is the fact that it would seem the community power complex appears, to a certain extent, as parallel to the institutional power structure of Córdoba; that is, as if it were not integrated into the other components of the power structure from the way in which some elements tend to integrate and others do not.

4. The top influentials participating in the power structure of Córdoba were 37 individuals, selected by judges from among 210 persons who were considered as influential. These 37 persons represented the following sectors:

Nine the business and finance sector
Six the government sector
Four the education sector (university professors)
Four the political parties sector
Three the independent professions sector
Three the religion sector
Three the mass communications sector
Two the military sector
One the labor sector
One the culture and art sector
One the entertainment or recreation sector

As seen from these figures, the top influentials tended to relate more to the community power complex than to the institutionalized power structure of Córdoba. Thus, it would seem that this component of the power structure rested upon informal grounds or, at least, on grounds which were not institutionalized and also to appear, like the power complex, in a form parallel to the institutionalized power structure of the community of Córdoba.

5. The key influentials of the community were fourteen persons who presented themselves as the leaders of the top influentials, according to their own statements, and with a high degree of accord, when it was a question of finding persons who effectively see that things are done in the community. These key influentials represented the following areas:

Six from the business and finance sector
Three from the education and independent professions sectors
Three from the government, political parties, and independent professions sectors
One from the mass communications and independent professions sectors
One from the society and wealth and (perhaps) independent professions sectors

From these data it is seen that the key influentials of the community represent business and finance in an overwhelming fashion (43%); also one notices the representation of three intimately interrelated sectors—education, independent professions, and political parties—which means that these key influentials have influence, through their multi-occupationality, in different sectors. It would appear that the university creates the possibility for leadership in different sectors, where the corresponding patterns of ruling groups are acquired, perhaps through the same formal preparation which is acquired (we will return to this later). From the figures one also sees another significant fact: the lack of key influentials in the religion, military, and labor sectors, which have been evaluated as sectors of great influence in the power structure of Córdoba, as we pointed out earlier. Also worth noting is the fact that there is an intimate interrelation between the top influentials and the key influentials, as well as an interrelation between the power complex and these influentials, something not occurring with the institutionalized power structure of the community. This allows affirmation that leadership appears in a segmented fashion according to the type of issue being discussed.

FIVE In the light of the data obtained, it would be fitting to analyze here the theory of the "interrelated components of the power structure" in Córdoba. In previous identification of the institutional structure of power in the global society and in the local community, one notes among these components of the community power structure a close interrelation in that on both levels one finds the same five institutional sectors as the most influential for getting things done in the community. The *test* of rank correlation of Spearman gives us a correlation of 0.84, which is significant enough. In turn, from the data obtained, it has been possible to verify that the influence of the military sector in getting things done in the community is greater on the national than local level; to some extent, this is fairly logical, although the importance it has is surprising, especially at the local level, if one compares it with the results obtained in the American or British cities to which we have alluded earlier. If we submit to the theory of C. Wright Mills, perhaps the importance of this sector at the level of national society in the modern and highly industrialized societies would not be surprising.[16]

The mass communications media sector has much more influence in the community than that ascribed in global society and, vice versa, the society and wealth sector has much more importance in global society than in the local community. The first fact may be owing to different circumstances which we will analyze later; the second, to a large degree, is intimately linked, at the national level, with the representation of the primary economic sector of the country, that is, representing the hacendados and estancieros and, certainly, with its organisms which have so much importance in the economy of the country; on the other hand, this economic sector is intimately linked to the society of Buenos Aires. In Córdoba, this society and wealth sector is currently of little importance in getting things done in the community.

The power complex of Córdoba reveals that the associations or interest groups tend to be a parallel component to the institutionalized power structure of the community; this would tend to demonstrate that this component is not institutionally integrated into the power structure. This fact is of great importance in determining the form of the power structure of Córdoba. Thus, it is noted that the business and finance, mass communications, and political parties sectors appear to have more influence in decisions taken in the community than that assigned to them by the institutional power structure. These sectors are more representative of a modern society, if we abide by the data we have on the other cities studied in the United States and England.

The top influentials of Córdoba show a high representation of the business and finance, government, education, and political parties sectors, although they also have importance in the independent professions, mass communications, and religion sectors. To a certain extent, this power component tends to integrate itself into the power complex, which, it would appear, influences this component of the power structure of Córdoba, notable in the high representation of the business and finance, mass communications, and political parties sectors in the power complex and among the top influentials; and it is very possible that the power complex influences the rise of certain sectors such as education and independent professions, owing to the multi-occupationality of the top influentials (to which we will return later). In any event, the top influentials represent both emerging and residual sectors, analyzed from the perspective of the industrial development of Córdoba. Here one notes that halo of a traditional city which Córdoba has in that the university (education sector) and the liberal professions (the doctors) are still sources of prestige which possess a famed technique for choosing the top influentials.

The key influentials show a structural profile similar to that of the top influentials and, to a great extent, to the power complex of Córdoba. But, further, it once again shows the parallelism of the power structure to the institutional form, since no ruling council, ecclesiastical hierarchy, or military chief appears among the key influentials, notwithstanding the high degree of influence attributed to the labor, religion, and military sectors in the institutional power structure of the community (labor fourth, religion first, and military fifth). Direct dependence upon orders emanating from a central power in these institutions results in these sectors creating no local leaders who get things done in the community; their influence is solely as an institutional sector, and individuals are important only for the representivity they confer within the institution organized in a bureaucratic and vertical manner. To some extent, it concerns sectors which are a little "federalistic."

The power structure of Córdoba, through the analysis made of the components of the power structure and of their interrelation, shows a lack of integration between the institutionalized forms of power and the noninstitutionalized forms of power (power complex, top influentials, and key influentials), these components moving in a parallel fashion in decisions taken in the community; on the one hand are found certain permanent components of the power structure (religion, military, and government sectors), and on the other are found certain emerging components (business and finance, mass communications, labor, and political parties sectors), and certain residual components (education, liberal professions, society and wealth sectors). Upon these latter rests the variability of the power structure of Córdoba if analyzed from the viewpoint of economic and social development; and, finally, from the perspective of the impact

102

of industrialization on the power structure of the community.

SIX The power structure of Córdoba shows, through everything exhibited, a nonintegrated form of its components as a result of the impact produced by the industrialization which occurred in Córdoba in the last few years. This would tend to show, on one hand, that the power structure of Córdoba is a result of the industrialization process and, on the other, that the present power structure of Córdoba is found in a condition of transition, since it has, contiguous and superimposed, permanent, emerging, and residual components. But perhaps most important is that it shows it has a tendency to structure itself in a definite fashion. To analyze this, we will observe, first, the institutional power structure of Córdoba around 1940 and compare it with the present institutional power structure of Córdoba.

The institutional power structure of Córdoba around 1940 distributed the sectors according to their influence in getting things done in the community, as follows:

1. Religion sector
2. Education sector
3. Independent professions sector
4. Government sector
5. Business and finance sector
6. Society and wealth sector
7. Military sector
8. Political parties sector
9. Mass communications sector
10. Labor sector
11. Culture and art sector
12. Social welfare sector
13. Entertainment and recreation sector

A simple comparison with the present institutionalized power structure shows us[17]: 1) that the religion, government, and, to a certain extent, the military sectors appear as permanent components of the power structure of Córdoba, with the well-known fact that the religion sector has been and still is in first place as a sector influential in decisions taken in the community; the same occurs with regard to the government sector at a lower level. The military sector shows an advance in position at present and this fact can be attributed to the new functions this sector currently fulfills in community decisions at the national level. (We will return to this later.) 2) The comparison also shows us that the business and finance, labor, and mass communications sectors have increased their influence in community decisions and that they are intimately tied to the industrial and technological development which occurred in Córdoba during the last years; it concerns the emerging sectors in the power structure of Córdoba. 3) And, finally, the comparison shows us that the education, independent professions, and society and wealth sectors have lost influence in decisions taken in the community and that they are generally fairly removed from the process of industrial and technological development which took place in Córdoba in recent years; it concerns residual sectors in the present power structure of Córdoba. The emerging sectors, to a certain degree, represent an industrial community and the residual sectors to some extent represent a traditional community.

Nevertheless, the power structure is not solely defined by the institutionalized power structure, upon which we make the comparison, but also by the power complex, the top influentials, and the key influentials. Although we do not have data to correlate these components, on the bases given, one can insinuate some conclusions, among which is noted the impact of the industrialization and technological processes occurring in Córdoba in the last years; in conclusion: the presence of traditional elements is noted in the power structure around 1940 and the presence of modern elements in the power structure now: but, and this is fundamental, one also notes the tendency for the power to structure itself into a definite form: "from industry to power."[18] The power structure of Córdoba in the present moment is a result of the process of industrialization which has taken place in this city during the last years.

SEVEN A comparative analysis of the power structure of Córdoba with that of the American or British cities to which we have made reference reveals[19] the presence of two sectors in Córdoba, military and religion, with a high degree of influence in decisions taken in the community, which are not found in the aforementioned American or British cities. These sectors, moreover, have a great importance both in the power structure of Córdoba around 1940 as well as at present. Therefore, we refer to these sectors as permanent components of the power structure of Córdoba. But, since these sectors are not very influential in the other cities, one must have an explanation regarding Córdoba, above all when it is seen that the influence of these sectors is only apparent when dealing with the institutionalized power structure both on the national and on the local level, and is not apparent when speaking of the power complex, the top influentials, and, above all, the key influentials of the community. We believe that only an historical view can explain this fact.

1. *The military sector in the power structure.* Since 1930 and during 34 years of Argentine history of the military sector, it has been, as is known, a very significant power force in the political life of the country, whether taking part actively and directly in the national government, or whether cunningly or indirectly influencing it. During this time, the military have revolted with success on four occasions, and have overthrown the established government; they have deposed as many dictatorial leaders as democratically elected presidents.

For more than ten years they have been in power with a de facto government, and for more than fifteen years they have been represented in the political government. At times they have won public approval for their actions and, at others, the most severe rebuff. The people have in general accepted this use of political power on the part of the military sector in the political life of the country only as a measure of extreme urgency. Popular demand favors a constitutional government with civilian representatives democratically elected.[20]

The presence of the military sector in the institutional power structure of the global society (in first place) and in the institutionalized power structure of the local community (in fifth place) plainly shows the interrelation of these levels; and the difference in the order of importance shows, to some extent, the dependence of the resolution of problems of national character. This dependence is based on a necessity of emergency (the national security) in the face of violation or threat of violation of certain norms or values held as unimpeachable in the country. Therefore, precisely, this emergency has arisen when concerned with international matters or when the Constitution was affected. Since the interests represented by the military sector are national ones, this sector must necessarily be represented in the community power structure, but, essentially, only as an institutional sector.

The permanent presence of the military sector in the community power structure, besides the reasons cited, can be due to the new functions this sector is fulfilling in local community life as, for example, with the manufacture of airplanes, the vehicle industry, etc., as well as with technical education, military education, etc. Therefore, this sector, even though it remains as permanent, tends to have more influence in the community, as it incorporates into the process of Cordobese economic, industrial, and technological development. But it is clear that these new functions do not justify the permanent presence of this sector in the community power structure, although it explains the growth of certain influence in other areas of the community. The permanent presence of the military sector in the power structure of Córdoba is based on the emergency power which it must inexorably discharge to satisfy its functions of national defense in a city of great importance in the life of the country, which perhaps the other cities studied (Seattle, Atlanta, and Bristol) did not have.

2. *The religion sector in the power structure.* The permanent presence of the religion sector in the power structure of Córdoba has, perhaps, very deep roots in the history of the city which go back to the times of the conquest and the Colony. Córdoba has always been considered a very Catholic city, which for a long time had not absorbed a foreign immigration that could disturb a generalized awareness of being an eminently Catholic population. On the other hand, the Catholic Church has played a very important role in the great historical events of the city, in past as well as in present times. But, above all, the Catholic Church has a legal indorsement of recognition which figures in the Constitution.

Nonetheless, there are other elements which can explain the permanence of this sector in the power structure of Córdoba, in spite of this sector not figuring highly represented in the power complex and not being represented adequately among the top influentials, and, above all, not having any representation among the key influentials.

An inventory and later analysis of the functions of the Catholic Church in Córdoba show, clearly, that its lines and channels of influence are considerable and fairly extensive. In effect, the Catholic Church in Córdoba has important functions and therefore decides in affairs of community interest in several sectors, such as business and finance, political parties, government, education, military, mass communications, labor, and social welfare. For this reason, perhaps, is this sector so important as an institutionalized sector, although it does not have the corresponding representation in other components of the power structure of Córdoba.

Because of these many functions fulfilled by the Catholic Church in Córdoba, the religion sector emerges as a very influential one in the community power structure, either directly and in institutionalized form as a sector, or indirectly and informally through the faithful Catholics who perform decisive functions in other sectors of the community life. The lack of sociometric leaders in the power structure and permanency in the power structure are owing to the traditional presence of the Church in the institutional power structure of the community, and which, on account of the multiple channels on which it relies to get things done in the community and owing to its multiple participation in different sectors, does not need key influentials. This traditional presence finds its support in the history of the city and in legal recognition as the official religion which has been sustained through the defense of its interests made by the same faithful Catholics who participate in the different institutional sectors of the power structure of Córdoba.

EIGHT A comparative analysis of the power structure of Córdoba with the power structure of the American and British cities to which we have referred, and a comparative analysis of the power structure of Córdoba around 1940 with the power structure of the city at present, reveals quite clearly that six sectors show variability in their degree of influence in succeeding in getting things done in the community. Three of these sectors—business and finance, labor, and mass communications—have gained influence in decisions taken in Córdoba; and three of these sectors—education, independent professions, and wealth and society—have lost influence in city decisions at present. Here one notes the impact of the process of industrialization and economic development. Nevertheless, in studying the composition and representivity of the top influentials and the key influentials, one notes the presence, contiguous and superimposed, of dual representatives of emerging and residual sectors, that is, a certain type of leadership with mixed criteria of a traditional and modern society. This fact, certainly, is not noted in the American and British cities studied, nor is it noted—and this we judge by approximation—in this component of Córdoba around 1940. Clearly, this requires an explanation, since this fact is perhaps the reason why the power structure of Córdoba does not have an integrated structure, that is, cohesively functional to encourage the process of industrial development, and as such, an indicator of a transitional type of power structure.

1. *Multi-occupationality of the top influentials.* The data collected in the empirical investigation have shown that of the 37 top influentials in Córdoba, 18 of them have two or more productive occupations of different type and participate in two or more sectors of the institutional structure of Córdoba. Thus one notices, for example, that university professorship (education sector), liberal professions (independent professions), political activity (government and political parties sectors), and journalistic activity (mass communications sector) are intimately linked in the activities of the top influentials. This multi-occupational superposition of the top influentials provides an activity duality in them, through which they participate in different institutional power sectors in influential positions to succeed in getting things done in the community. These circumstances have a double repercussion in the constitution of the power structure: on one hand, it tends not to exhibit activity specialization, making it seem a demand and a necessity of a process of development, and on the other hand, it tends not to exhibit community activities when concerning projects or matters of general interest. This double repercussion attributable to the multi-occupationality of the top influentials of Córdoba does not appear in the other cities studied. Therefore, it gives the power structure of the community a very characteristic profile: for one, the top influentials appear from a certain personal prestige; for

another, they tend to have a relative influence in succeeding to get things done in the community, but they do not participate in community activities, that is, in committees or voluntary associations formed to get things done in the community; to a certain degree, the top influentials, by their constitution, place a premium on such criteria as prestige over criteria of effectiveness.

2. *Formal preparation of the top influentials.* A fairly significant and differentiating characteristic of the top influentials of Córdoba with respect to those of the American and British cities is the degree and type of their formal preparation. The majority have a professional university training. This fact, it is useful to point out, is closely connected to the multi-occupationality of the top influentials.

The university graduates among the top influentials of Córdoba represented the following professions:

Ten lawyers
Five engineers
Two physicians
Two architects
Two priests
Two army officials
Four universitarians

The top influentials, consequently, who have university preparation, are 27 out of 37; the ten remaining do not have university backgrounds. From these figures one discovers, as a fairly plausible fact, that the professional university training gives the top influentials a non-specialized view of the institutional sectors in which they participate and, at the same time, gives the top influentials different opportunities in the most diverse sectors of the institutional life of the community. It would seem that university preparation equips them for "everything," above all considering the high percentage of liberal professions (lawyers, physicians, engineers, and architects) among the top influentials who take part in the government, political parties, business and finance, education, and mass communications sectors.

At all events, the degree and type of professional training of the top influentials turns out to be highly significant in Córdoba, granted that perhaps they base their leadership on reasons of prestige and not on effectiveness in community activities. These facts are residual characteristics inserted into emerging sectors closely tied to the process of industrial development of the city.

3. *Political activity of the top influentials.* The data obtained showed a large number of political leaders among the top influentials, a fact which certainly is not present in the other cities studied. The multi-party system, such as appears in Argentina, no doubt tends to increase the number of persons participating in political activity. It is not the moment to analyze the causes for the existence of this legal structure, but rather to seek an explanation for the presence of so many political leaders among the top influentials of Córdoba. One fact appears as clear: the lack of very marked majorities, grouped around two or three parties, as occurs in the United States and in Britain, always creates the possibility of having to rely on the leaders of other parties for future coalitions or for the approval of projects or matters of direct community interest; hence, the always potential necessity of counting on the leaders of the most varied political parties because, at a given moment, they can play a decisive role in decisions taken in the community. This fact, in turn, underscores the multi-occupationality of the political leaders, who do not necessarily live from political activity, among other reasons because of the changing political situations of the last years and for want of a political professionalization of the leaders in each party. These facts, to a great extent, correspond to residual characteristics in the composition of the top influentials. The continual political changes in Argentina during the last years have encouraged a constant advancement of political leaders, many of whom have never

performed professionally in the political parties sector nor in the government sector; to participate in the political sectors it is not necessary to be a professional politician and, even less, a specialist. A certain personal prestige, some university professional preparation, and a certain amount of promotion by means of the mass communications media will usually be sufficient to be a politician.

NINE A comparative analysis of the present power structure of Córdoba and its power structure around 1940 shows, as we have pointed out on several occasions, that the business and finance, labor, and mass communications sectors emerge as influential in decisions taken in the community. It would seem that these three sectors are closely tied to the industrial and technological development Córdoba is undergoing, above all if one analyzes the sectors which are losing influence: education, independent professions, and society and wealth. Now we should like to analyze the emerging sectors, especially business and finance and labor, which would seem the most connected to the industrialization process. Nevertheless, these institutionalized sectors present certain incongruities when the top influentials and key influentials of the community are analyzed. Thus, we find the business and finance sector is highly represented among the top influentials and key influentials of the community; nevertheless, the labor sector is scarcely once represented among the top influentials and never represented among the key influentials. These facts, certainly, call for an explanation, since in some way they show the state in which the power structure of Córdoba is found. Perhaps it is one more indication of the state of transition and the tendency the power structure shows in the form it is acquiring:

1. *The labor leaders in the power structure.* The importance of this institutional sector in decisions taken in the community is sufficiently evident, since it occupies fourth place in the order of importance; in turn, it has representation

in the community power complex. Nonetheless, this sector has only one representative among the top influentials and none among the key influentials of the community. Perhaps reasons of an historical and structural nature can explain this fact. With respect to the former, it would be useful to point out that since the Peronista epoch the advancement of labor leaders corresponded to personal motives, closely bound to the caprice of the political leader par excellence of the working class. The newness of the syndicate movement, which dates from some 20 years, has favored this system of promotion of labor leaders since there was no time to train capable leaders, nor did legal tools exist which would permit of this training. Perhaps the sanction of the Law of Professional Associations created, for the first time, the possibility of preparing labor leaders. It would seem that at present the situation can change; because the evident fact is that labor leaders still have not become integrated as top influentials into the power structure of Córdoba. On the other hand, the vertical and centralized organization of Argentine trade unionism does not favor the promotion of labor leaders at a local or community level; at best, it favors the promotion of labor leaders at national level. This type of organization, besides, creates dependence on the decisions of orders emanating from the central organisms, almost without an autonomy of decision at local or community level. We believe these two facts can explain the importance this sector has as an institutional sector in decisions taken in the community and the importance it is acquiring with the industrial development of Córdoba and, at the same time, the lack of representation of this sector among the top influentials and key influentials of the community; a fact, certainly, which does not appear in the American and British cities studied. Nevertheless, the trend shows the increasing importance this sector will have in all components of the power structure of Córdoba while the process of industrial development of the community continues, since it tends to advance this sector parallel to the business and finance sector.

2. *The influentials of the business and finance sector.* The importance of this institutional sector in decisions taken in the community is evident enough, since it occupies second place in the order of importance; in turn, it has evident representation in the community power complex. But, and this is quite important, it has a high representation among the top influentials and key influentials of the community. Perhaps historical reasons, given the recency of the impact of the industrialization process on the power structure, explain this fact. Nonetheless, there are certain functional incongruities which perhaps cause this sector not to have full strength in the community power structure, since this sector tends to promote as top influentials and as key influentials persons or representatives of other institutional sectors of the community, such as independent professions and, to a certain extent, society and wealth. The explanation of this incongruity is due, in part, to the fact that much of the capital upon which this sector rests is foreign capital, or rather, that the executives of the most important industrial enterprises are foreign citizens. This fact, in itself, evident in Córdoba, makes the foreign executives, in order to succeed in getting something done in the community, resort to national figureheads who enjoy a certain prestige in the community. These figureheads, in general, represent the independent professional and the society and wealth sectors. In turn, they promote themselves as top influentials and as key influentials or representatives of other sectors which serve the interests of the business and finance sector. This, to a great extent, would explain the presence of so many professionals among the key influentials. Nevertheless, this promotion of leaders in the community who belong to the independent professions and to society and wealth has a double repercussion: on one hand it tends to include among the influentials representatives of sectors which are residual to some extent and, on the other, tends to modernize, especially in the independent professions

sector, since the professionals tend to incorporate themselves into the company bureaucracy, abandoning the free exercise of a profession; finally: it is a question of bureaucratizing the liberal professions. Therefore, certainly, this sector—which is small—tends to incorporate into the process of industrial development of the community. This explains to a large extent the functional incongruity of the business and finance sector in the power structure of Córdoba by this dual character in the promotion of the top influentials and key influentials of the community.

Besides, the functional incongruity of the business and finance sector in the power structure of Córdoba is borne out by the recency of the industrialization process in that this sector, when based on national capital, arises from commerce and light industry which, for various reasons, has entered the industrialization process. Therefore, in the industrialization process of Córdoba one notes the contiguous and superimposed presence of traditional and modern enterprises.[21] From this emerge patterns for the promotion of leaders which still correspond to criteria of a traditional society. Among these leaders are now found representatives of the independent professions and the society and wealth sectors. This fact strengthens the repercussion of foreign capital, or rather, of the foreign executives, in the advancement of residual sectors of the power structure of Córdoba.[22]

These functional incongruities point up the state of transition of the power structure of Córdoba, since the business and finance sector is one of those, in all its components of the power structure, which has a strong influence in getting things done in the community. The trend, nevertheless, tends to secure this sector in the power structure of Córdoba.

TEN A comparative analysis of the power structure of Córdoba around 1940, as we have already said, points up the loss of influence of three sectors: education, society and wealth, and independent professions. The first went from 2nd to 7th place; the second from 6th to 9th place; and the third from 3rd to 10th place. Nevertheless, among the top influentials and among the key influentials, one notes the presence of persons representing these sectors in the community power structure. We have already said something, in part, about the independent professions sector; therefore, we will touch upon it only when analyzing the other sectors which, at present, we consider more representative of residual sectors. We repeat, we use this expression in a functional sense regarding the industrial development of Córdoba, that is, since they tend to resist (instead of encourage) this process.

1. *The social function of the university.* The education sector is represented, preeminently, by the university as a social institution. For various historical reasons, the National University of Córdoba has fulfilled a very efficient social function for many years and in different historical moments; normally it has always been involved in the great events occurring in the city and has influenced decisions taken in the community. It would seem that at present the National University of Córdoba does not influence decisions taken in the city, at least if we abide by the data just assembled; to around 1940, to the contrary, the university was a source of power and influenced community decisions. This is a fact requiring an explanation.

There is no doubt that education, above all, professional and technical education, is one of the more important factors in industrial development and, as such, is one of the major inciting factors of the process of economic and social development. Nevertheless, it would seem that the University of Córdoba is not integrated into the development process which is occurring in the community. And, to the contrary, it would seem that the University of Córdoba, around 1940, was integrated into the community. At least this is what is inferred from the collected data. Finally, this signifies lack of actuality; that is, lack of fulfilling the social function which the university possesses by definition as an institution. This lack of actuality would be manifest: a) in the educational content; b) in the social objectives of the university, and c) in the performance of the personnel, whether teaching staff or students. Certain information would demonstrate the obviousness of these assertions. To this fact must be added the updating of the organization of this same university to answer to the massive weight of its student population, an action demanded by a process of industrialization. At present we will not deal with the university problem, but only seek an explanation for the loss of its influence in decisions taken in the community for lack of this updating, that is, for not fulfilling its social function which, ultimately, is to satisfy the exigencies and demands of the industrialization process.

The presence of top influentials and key influentials representing the education sector can only be explained by the prestige which the old university institution still conveys; but it is not owing to the efficiency of these people in formulating and carrying out decisions taken in Córdoba. We believe that these simple facts can explain the presence of the education sector in the power structure of Córdoba through the top influentials who normally are university products. At present, owing to diverse internal causes (organization, lack of action, lack of investigation, etc.), the education sector, and especially the university, constitutes a residual element of the power structure of Córdoba. For fundamental reasons, this contradiction will have to be overcome in the near future.

2. *The society and wealth sector as a ruling class.* The loss of influence of this sector in decisions taken in the community is evident enough. Nevertheless, as we have seen, in the national order this sector still carries its importance in the institutional power structure. This sector, to a great extent, represents the traditional social groups, the old families of

Córdoba. These families based their power, among other things, on the primary sector of the economy, that is, on the land. Towards 1940 the economy of Córdoba perhaps still supported itself from returns of the land; industrial growth channeled the wealth of the city into industry and commerce, and thus new people had economic control of the city; concurrently, this sector also lost control of the wealth of the land. This fact, to be sure, does not occur at the national level, where the society and wealth sector still controls the power of the main sector of the national economy. This explains why the society and wealth sector is influential at the national level and very little at the local level. As such, the society and wealth sector has remained, in the power structure of Córdoba, as a residual element which does not participate in the economic and social development of Córdoba.

Following the trend, this sector will slowly disappear as an institutional sector and perhaps will incorporate into other institutional power sectors in the future: business and finance, independent professions, etc. At present, and since it still has representatives among the top influentials, this sector constitutes, perhaps uniquely, a prestige factor which "bedecks" the new groups arisen from the process of industrial development; the renowned techniques in the selection of top influentials allow the incorporation of representatives of this institutional sector into the power structure of Córdoba, but perhaps as residues of a traditional society which still exhibits certain elements with strength, above all, if one keeps in mind the novelty the process of industrialization has for Córdoba, and which as yet has not consumed certain values of social prestige.

ELEVEN The general conclusion we draw from all the data presented and explanations given is that the power structure of Córdoba is not integrated, that is, its components show certain functional inconsistencies in the industrial

FIGURE 1

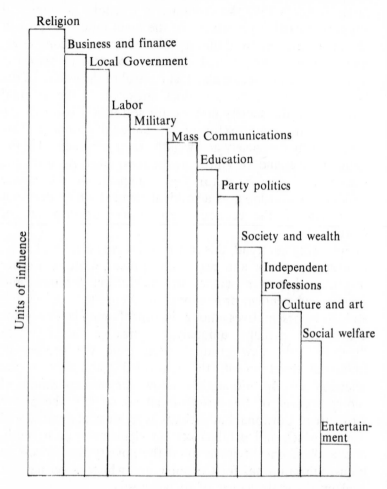

These gradations were set up in units of influence by conversion of rank given each by an informant. This conversion was made giving first place to units given a rank of 13, second place to rank of 12, and diminishing down to 13th place, which received a rank of 1. Each classification given by the informants in each group was obtained for each sector using the formula: $f(13) + f(12) + f(11) + f(10) + f(9) + f(8) + f(7) + f(6) + f(5) + f(4) + f(3) + f(2) + f(1)$.

power structure is not controlled by a group of individuals who have all the power and who use it in a standard fashion to achieve some objective, consciously or unconsciously defined. But the fact that no power elite exists at present does not imply that power does not have a structure in Córdoba; there is a transitional structure. This assertion has been verified in this work—at least, we hope so.

In effect, the data obtained have shown us: a) that the institutional power structure of the global society is intimately linked to the institutional structure of the community; b) that the power complex is structured in a form parallel to the institutional power structure, and c) that the top influentials and key influentials exhibit residual elements of an old power structure and emerging elements of a new power structure which tends to come together as a whole. The interrelation of these components of the power structure indicates a nonintegrated (or informally integrated) power structure as a result of the social dynamics imposed by the process of industrialization of Córdoba. This nonintegration of the power structure appears in a conflicting form and, therefore, as the motor of the dynamics of the development of the community. The conflict appears between the residual and emerging elements of the power structure, which emphasizes the transitional state of its structure and the tendency to structure itself in a definite way. Therefore, at present, given the conflictive state of two systems, a power elite does not appear; and given the state of trend towards imposition of a system over everything, the possibility arises of formation in the future of a power elite. But in order for this to occur, it is necessary that the process which defines the tendency remains constant and progressive, that is, the industrialization process. And this is a problem of politics. But also it is necessary that a certain degree of stability be achieved in the community social structures, that is, a definite state of development. And this, also, is a problem of politics.

122

The identity of social class among the power-holders in Córdoba can bring credence to the existence of invisible coalitions which define an elite; but a) the diversified segmentation of power sectors throws doubt on the presence of a standard behavior of those individuals to achieve an objective, consciously or unconsciously defined; and, in turn b) the rare participation of the top influentials in voluntary associations hinders agreement, knowingly or unknowingly, on common objectives.[23] But, on the other hand, the gradual strength and diffusion of the patterns imposed by a sector or various sectors which set the process of industrialization into motion can create the conditions which would tend to overcome in Córdoba the diversified segmentation of the power sectors and the lack of participation in voluntary associations, since the industrialization process can achieve, through an "elective affinity" (Max Weber), an adaptation or adjustment of the economically relevant structures (in our case, the power structure) to the economic structures. When such adjustment or adaptation is achieved—and the tendency is towards this—it is very possible that a power elite will be formed in Córdoba; but—as we have already said—for this to occur it is necessary that the process of industrialization remain constant and progressive and that the state of the power structure be overcome.

THIRTEEN We have attempted to maintain in this work that the power elites can be functionally defined only as a state of the society or the community and as a trend of development; anything else can be no more than mere supposition or political prejudice. Any stable society or community tends functionally to have a power elite, whatever the criteria defining this elite, which certainly can be many and varied. And, to the contrary, any society or community in transition will functionally tend not to have a power elite, whatever may be the defining criteria. The power structure, then, always appears in a community or society because the relation of power and the division of social work are constants of all the known past and present societies. The form in which that power structure appears depends on the state of the society and the trend of its development. The power structure of Córdoba currently appears to be without a power elite (being a non-integrated structure), but it can again have one (when it once more integrates). According to the type of society to which it tends (or aspires), so will be the form in which this power elite integrates itself. The city of Córdoba, at present, tends to be integrating an elite of a definite type which will control all the power: "from industry to power"!

APPENDIX II
Governors of Córdoba
(1916-1967)

1916—Eufrasio Loza
   (Radical)
1917—Julio C. Borda
   (Radical)*
1919—Rafael Núñez
   (Democrat)
1921—Jerónimo del
   Barco
   (Democrat)*
1922—Julio A. Roca

   (Democrat)
1925—Ramón J.
   Cárcano
   (Democrat)

1928—José Antonio
   Ceballos
   (Radical)*
1930—Basilio Pertiné
   (Federal intervener)
1930—Carlos Ibarguren
   (Federal intervener)

1931—Enrique Torino
   (Federal intervener)

1932—Emilio F. Olmos
   (Democrat)
1932—Pedro J. Frías
   (Democrat)*

1936—Julio Torres
(Democrat)*
1936—Luis Funes
(Democrat)*
1936—Amadeo Sabatini
(Radical)
1940—Santiago H.
del Castillo
(Radical)
1943—Justo Salazar
Collado
(Federal intervener)
1943—León S. Scasso
(Federal intervener)
1944—Alberto Guglielmone
(Federal intervener)
1944—Juan Carlos Díaz
Cisneros
(Federal intervener)
1945—Hugo A. Oderigo
(Federal intervener)
1946—Argentino Auchter
(Peronista)
1947—Román A. Subiza
(Federal intervener)
1947—Aristóbulo Vargas
Belmonte
(Federal intervener)
1949—Alfredo M.
Eguzquiza
(Federal intervener)
1949—Juan Ignacio

San Martín
(Peronista)
1951—Atilio Antinucci
(Peronista)
1952—Raúl Felipe Lucini
(Peronista)
1955—Dalmiro Videla
Balaguer
(Federal intervener)
1956—Medardo Gallardo
Valdés
(Federal intervener)
1958—Arturo O. Zanichelli
(UCRI)
1960—Francisco Antonio
de Larrechea
(Federal intervener)
1962—Jorge Bermúdez
Emparanza
(Federal intervener)
1962—Mario I. Atencio
(Federal intervener)
1962—Aniceto Pérez
(Federal intervener)
1962—Rogelio Nores
Martínez
(Federal intervener)
1964—Justo Páez
Molina
(Radical)
1966—Gustavo Martínez
Zubiría
(Federal intervener)

1966—Miguel Ángel   1967—Carlos José
      Ferrer Deheza   Caballero
      (Governor?)   (Governor?)

The names marked with an asterisk (*) are of Vice-Governors, who for various reasons (death, resignation, etc.), replaced the Governor until the end of the term; in 1936 there were three Vice-Governors who were Governor through various institutional reasons.

APPENDIX III
The Sampling

1—Julio A. Roca
2—Félix Sarría
3—Guillermo Rothe
4—Daniel E. Gavier
5—Rodolfo Martínez
6—Facundo Escalera
7—Alfredo Malbrán
8—Eufrasio Loza
9—Pedro Larlús
10—Augusto Funes
11—Manuel S. Ordóñez
12—Manuel Astrada
13—Juan F. Cafferata
14—Mariano P. Ceballos
15—Rubén Dussaut
16—Daniel Fernández
17—Julián Maidana
18—José H. Martínez
19—Eduardo Quinteros
20—Arturo M. Bas
21—Federico Iturraspe Cabot
22—Manuel Peña
23—Ramón J. Cárcano
24—Eduardo Duffy
25—Pedro Moreno
26—Pedro Loustau Bidaut
27—José María Martínez
28—Ernesto Romagoza
29—León S. Morra
30—José C. Lazcano
31—Luis Achával
32—Henoch Aguiar
33—Guillermo Rothe
34—Enrique Martínez Paz
35—Pedro S. Rovelli
36—Sofanor Novillo Corbalán

37—Guillermo Rothe
38—Félix Sarría
39—José María Valdez
40—Juan B. González
41—Santiago Díaz
42—Rafael Moyano
43—Félix J. Molina
44—Horacio Oulton
45—José del Viso
46—Belisario Martínez
47—Moisés Escalante
48—José María Valdez
49—Juan B. González
50—Augusto Casas
51—Medardo Álvarez
     Luque
52—Aurelio E. Crespo
53—Juan José Garaventa
54—Gorgonio Isla Racedo
55—Federico Iturraspe
     Cabot
56—Miguel Juárez
57—Carlos I. Luque
58—Hipólito Montagné
59—Francisco Oliva
60—Santos Ortiz
61—Edelmiro Pérez
62—Francisco Roca
63—Jorge Torres Castaños
64—Julio Torres
65—Antenor de la Vega
     Luque
66—Ernesto Zeppa
67—Abel Granillo Barros
68—Amadeo Sabattini

69—Alejandro Gallardo
70—Santiago H. del
     Castillo
71—Augustín Garzón
     Agulla
72—Antonio Medina
     Allende
73—Alfredo Larrosa
74—Tristán Paz Casas
75—Donato Latella Frías
76—Julio A. Roca
77—Miguel Ángel Cárcano
78—Ramón J. Cárcano
79—Justiniano Allende
     Posse
80—Mariano P. Ceballos
81—José H. Martínez
82—Guillermo Rothe
83—Américo Aguilera
84—Juan F. Cafferata
85—Carlos D. Courel
86—Juan Carlos Agulla
87—Facundo Escalera
88—Damián Fernández
89—Marcial Zarazaga
90—Elloy Illáñez
91—Amleto Magris
92—Gregorio N. Martínez
93—Bernardo Movsichoff
94—Ernesto Peña
95—Néstor Pizarro
96—Benito Soria
97—Teobaldo Zabala Ortiz
98—Sofanor Novillo
     Corbalán

99—Guillemo Stucker
[Guillermo?]
100—Julio de Tezanos Pinto
101—Manuel Augusto
Ferrer
102—Enrique Martínez Paz
103—Carlos Oliva Vélez
104—Enrique Martínez Paz
105—Pedro Clara
106—Aurelio E. Crespo
107—Sofanor Novillo
Corbalán
108—José Manuel Álvarez
109—José Cortés Funes
110—Jorge Díaz
111—Macelino Espinosa
112—Miguel Escalante
Echague
113—Rodolfo Garzón Funes
114—Victor N. Romero del
Prado
115—Diógenes Ruiz
116—Juan Vexenat
117—Domingo Yáñez
Álvarez
118—Juan C. Álvarez
Igarzábal
119—José Basso
120—Ezio Bellone
121—Cirilo Carranza
122—Alberto Castro
123—Juan Carlos
Christensen
124—Roberto Díaz
125—José Ferreyra Vázquez

126—Anselmo Funes
127—Luis Funes
128—Arturo U. Illia
129—Manuel Jofré Flores
130—Justo R. Loza
131—Ovidio Marcuzzi
132—Osvaldo Mariano
133—Alfredo S. Miles
134—Daniel Morra
135—Oscar Oyhamburo
136—José Piattini
137—Laureano Pizarro
138—Sinforiano Prado
139—Antonio S. Rivarola
140—Vincente Torres
141—Pascual Zanotti
142—Oscar S. Santucho
143—Rodolfo Bustos
144—Julio Torres
145—Gustavo A. Figueroa
146—Juan I. San Martín
147—Atilio Antinucci
148—Augustín Lascano
Pizarro
149—Pedro Baggio
150—Juan M. Castro Justo
151—Francisco J. Vocos
152—Victor Sandrín
153—Pablo López
154—Erio A. Bonetto
155—José Romariz
156—Lucas I. de Olmos
157—José B. Posadas
158—Osvaldo Amelotti
159—Felipe Gómez del Junco

160—Luis Atala
161—Raúl Busto Fierro
162—Arturo U. Illia
163—Raúl F. Lucini
164—José Maldonado Lara
164—Juan E. Montes
166—Luis Alberto Pereyra
167—Pedro Sánchez
168—Mauricio Yadarola
169—Miguel A. Zabala Ortiz
170—Mateo de Urtiaga
   Bilbao
171—Isidoro Varea
172—Natalio Treviño
173—Enrique Martínez
   Luque
174—José M. Urrutia
175—Lisardo Novillo
   Saravia

176—Ricardo Smith
177—Pedro Fontana
178—José Verna
179—Rodolfo Laje
   Weskamp

180—Severo Reinoso
181—Carlos A. Berardo
182—Pablo Mariconde
183—Raúl Cuestas Garzón
184—José I. Esteve
185—Carlos J. Portela
186—Luis Achával
187—Gustavo Carranza
188—Horacio Ahumada
189—Pedro G. Altamira
190—Carlos Moyano Centeno

191—Alejandro Vieyra
192—Hilario Martínez
193—Antonio de la Rúa
194—Luis A. Luque
195—Raúl Lazcano
   Colodrero
196—Pedro S. Spina
197—Rafael Buteler
   Echenique
198—Rodolfo Ordóñez
199—Helio Olmos
200—Eufrasio Loza (h.)
201—Alfredo Magaldi
202—Ricardo Tillard
203—Emilio Zanón
204—Guillermo Martínez
   Díaz
205—Guillermo Becerra
   Oliva
206—Raúl González Palau
207—Raúl Álvarez
208—Alberto Chávez
209—Antonio Cornejo
210—José Inaudi
211—Mario Sársfield Otero
212—Narciso Aguero Díaz
213—Ivo Hiram Pepe
214—Luis G. Martínez
   Villada
215—Martínez Romero
216—José Posadas
217—Pedro Albertini
218—José M. Barreyro
219—Ángel B. Brunetti
220—Santiago Cámara
221—Eugenio Candia

222—Leopoldo Caro
223—Adolfo Cividanes
224—Carlos Gallo
225—Tomás García Vieyra
226—Félix Krug
227—Cruz Lascano
228—José R. López
229—José A. Loza
230—Juan B. Borsani
231—Juan F. Funes
232—Ernesto Lobos
 Castellanos
233—Justo R. Magnasco
234—Carlos Martínez Casas
235—Manuel M. Moreno
236—Héctor J. Moyano
237—Luis N. Moyano
 Trebucq
238—Pedro Ochoa

239—Julio Salusso
240—José Saumell
241—Ignacio Ugarte
242—Federico de Uña
243—J. F. Villagra Mías
244—Arturo Zanichelli
245—Delfino Zemme
246—Arturo Zanichelli
247—Angel Reale
248—Félix Martín
249—Pedro Albertini
250—Miguel Paschetta
251—José V. Bertarelli
252—Azucena B. de
 Vaschetto

253—Hugo Vaca Narvaja

254—Héctor J. Panzeri
255—Héctor Moyano
256—Abelardo Recalde
 Funes
257—Gilberto H. Molina
258—Francisco J. Melani
259—Héctor E. Figueroa
260—Enrique Nores
 Martínez
261—Pedro J. Frías (h.)

262—José Schamiss
263—Fermín Alarcia
264—Rufino Alvarez
265—Héctor Angaroni
266—Miguel Barretto
267—Enrique Bauducco
268—Carlos Alberto Becerra
269—Julio A. Brower de
 Konig
270—José García Flores
271—Rafael Hernández
 Ramírez

272—Juan Raúl López
273—Juan Antonio Mas
274—Ricardo A. Montes
275—Mario Roberto
276—Pedro J. Sujeros
277—Hugo Storani
278—Salvador Valle
279—José Luis Vesco
280—Enrique Mario Znny
281—Jorge Orgaz
282—Benjamín Cornejo
283—Alfredo Acuña
284—Juan Martín Allende

285—Francisco Yunyent
286—Filemón Castellanos
 Posse
287—Raúl Bulgheroni
288—Luis A. Rébora
289—Adelmo R.
 Montenegro
290—Servando García Faure
291—Jorge Camargo
292—Jean Sonet
293—Ángel S. Segura
294—Agustín Díaz Bialet
295—Luis Aguero Pinero
296—Alberto Laserre
297—Víctor M. Contreras
298—Julio Pinzani
299—Ricardo Núñez
300—Esteban Gorriti
301—Pedro Oviedo Jocou
302—Antonio de la Rúa
303—Jorge Gómez Franco
304—Saúl González
305—Alberto López
 Carusillo
306—Celestino Piotti
307—Armando Pedernera
308—Raúl Torres Bas
309—José A. Luque
310—Alejandro Moyano
311—Carlos Lascano
312—Eduardo Ordóñez
313—Juan Claudio Villalba
314—Arturo Cabrera
315—Roberto Oliva
 Carreras
316—Raúl Álvarez

317—Guillermo Becerra
 Oliva
318—Stanislao Fiestas
319—Juan Carlos Roca
320—Lázaro Casacow
321—Alberto Ferser
 Moyano
322—Domingo Funes
 Guesalaga
323—Carlos Cony
324—Oscar Turcchi
325—Jaime Klinger
326—Aníbal Ojeda Gómez
327—Arturo Echenique
328—Carlos Moyano Centeno
329—Hipólito Artetas
330—Jesús Cabanillas
331—Abel Ardiles
332—Alberto Chávez
333—Eduardo Martínez
 Echenique
334—Osvaldo Tomatis
335—Juan Paschetta
336—Néstor Álvarez
 Cordeiro
337—Oscar Roqué Núñez
338—Bernardo Soto
339—Carlos J. Caballero
340—Osvaldo Tarditti
341—Miguel Moyano
 Centeno
342—Raúl Alfonso
343—Pedro Barciocco
344—Horacio Barreyro
345—Pedro Bertorello Rosa
346—Raúl Pedro Bizet

347—Leandro Boaglio
348—Oscar Bonino
349—Oscar Bosicovich
350—Francisco Cornavaca
351—Eugenio Conde
352—Fernando Cachau
353—Alberto Danguy
354—Fernando Díaz Cornejo
355—Oscar Durrieux
356—José Ferreiro
357—José Funes
358—David Indiveri
359—Francisco Revero
360—Pedro Vecchio
361—Marcelo Torres
362—Neyef Sucaría

363—Noberto Spertino
364—Ricardo Serafini
365—Cosme Saravia
366—Víctor H. Martínez
367—José Antonio Mecado
368—Alfredo Minichetti
369—Rodolfo Monguillot
370—Pedro Nicolato
371—José Olmedo
372—Oscar Alfredo Olsen
373—Carlos Pallavecini
374—Héctor J. Panzeri
375—Hipólito Quigan
376—José Rafaelli
377—Ramón Ramírez
378—Santiago Re Crespo

APPENDIX IV

Methodology of the Investigation

Access to empirical data, in an investigation of this type, is always very difficult for reasons that are very easy to understand, among which distrust is not far removed. In our investigation, this task was made harder by the long period encompassed by the object of our investigation, since it involved the study of more than fifty years of the life of Córdoba and, particularly, of the political life of the city. And the political history of Córdoba of the last fifty years is not written. We had to work on the basis of unedited documents (newspaper accounts, narratives, reminiscences, etc.), and from some partial studies on aspects of life of the city; nevertheless, the main source of data we found in information from the very players in the process, whom we

personally interviewed. In this way an extensive background
was immediately obtained for the later analysis of data, for
their organization, and for the original statement of the
pattern of investigation.

Later an extensive study was made of the bibliography on
the subject in Spanish (especially in Argentina), English,
French, and German. The actual bibliography, certainly, was
not large. Two areas claimed our attention: the problem of
the elites and the problem of social stratification. Two
seminars were held in the Faculty of Philosophy and
Humanities of the National University of Córdoba in 1967;
the first, on the theory and existing investigations on social
stratification and elites and, the second, on the investigations
on social stratification and elites carried out in Argentina and
Latin America. The general conclusion reached from these
theoretical studies was that in a transitional society, there
exist, contiguous and superimposed, at least two systems of
social stratification, one of which appears as residual and the
other as emerging in the face of the process of industrial
development. Consequently, it was to be foreseen that in a
society such as Argentina, and in a community such as
Córdoba, at present both residual and emerging social strata
would have to appear. It was also clear in these studies that
the process of industrial development tends to produce a
definite system of social stratification which appears as a
result of the type and form of social mobility which the
process engenders. (Cf. Juan Carlos Agulla, *Razón y
sociedad,* Tucumán, National University of Tucumán, 1965.)

As soon as realized, this theoretical stage was entered into
the pattern of investigation; it was found to be simple and
flexible. Therefore, we took as point of departure the
conclusions drawn in our study on the power structure of
Córdoba, that appeared in the book: *De la industria al poder*
(Buenos Aires: Ediciones Libera, 1966); in the work:
"Córdoba: poder y desarrollo", *Aportes* (Paris, No. 2,

October 1966), pp. 80-105; and, in part, in the book: *Centralismo y federalismo* (Buenos Aires: Ediciones Libera, 1967). The investigation sought to continue these studies on the power structure.

Further, a listing was made of the people who, in three institutional sectors—politics, judicial, and university—had occupied the highest institutional hierarchies (governors, vice-governors, provincial ministers, chiefs of police, national ministers, national senators, national deputies, provincial senators, officials of the City of Córdoba, members of the Superior Court of Justice, members of the Supreme Council, rectors, vice-rectors, and deans of the universities). This listing, after several attempts and deliberations—explained at the beginning of this work—was reduced to those who had occupied these posts in four key years: 1924, 1937, 1951 and 1960. The selection of these years is explained in Chapter I. As it was our intention to observe a trend and not to make a description, we believed that this demand would be satisfied through the key years.

Each key year corresponded to an historical period, clearly distinguished by a revolution, with governments of different parties and ideologies, which spanned about one vital generation (approximately 12 years). From this list it was necessary to extract the people belonging to the Cordobese aristocracy to obtain from them the data we needed. This was simple and objective; there were no opinions. Questionnaires sent out to these people were filled in; many of them were sent by mail, others were filled in by the author (or an aide) in a personal conversation with the person concerned, and others were filled in by relatives when the parties had died, which certainly were many, especially for the first periods analyzed. All these data were submitted to proof of verification made by informants. All the necessary data were obtained.

Nevertheless, the great problem we had was the selection of the sampling, that is, to know who were the members of the

Cordobese aristocracy. To solve this problem—of difficult solution in the theoretical field—we resorted, on the one hand, to a theoretical-operative statement, and on the other to the help of key informants who acted as evaluators. The theoretical-operative statement consisted of defining the Cordobese aristocracy through those who held power before 1918 or perhaps 1916; these ruling *élites* had to represent the entire social stratum, since they themselves exercised control of all the power of the city and did so in a manner standard to the stratum. After the Sáenz Peña Law, the first institutionalized mechanism was set up for exchange of the ruling elites and, therefore, the Cordobese aristocracy necessarily had to share the power with other social strata. Consequently, the definition was given through a description of the Cordobese aristocracy before 1918. This was obtained through documents and studies made on Córdoba at the beginning of the century.

The key informants were a group of 16 persons who possessed the conditions and characteristics of this description, many of them being active in the power structure of the city at that time; half were men and half were women; the ages of the evaluators varied, since it was sought to have them represent the different historical periods being analyzed. The selection made by this group, done on an individual basis, was unanimous (with rare exceptions). The evaluation was made in a spontaneous manner and in conversations with the author.

All the conversations were noted down, since they served as a control for these evaluations. The evaluations were made during informal conversations and embraced different aspects of the life of Córdoba. Many of these evaluators were quite old (some more than 80). The memory and richness of details furnished by these people deserve the highest praise. Some of these conversations—and by special request of these individuals—were conducted in a group, in order to "better remember." It would be almost impossible to express how much this work owes to these evaluators. I remain deeply grateful to them. The later work, after a comparison and control of the information, was merely mechanical.

We are perfectly aware that the methodology used and the technique for obtaining the data can be defective; nonetheless, they met our needs. We were not trying here to make methodological preciosities, but to obtain real information. And I believe we succeeded. May the ethics of the investigator endorse the objectivity with which this work has been carried out.

Notes

Chapter I

1. D.C. Miller, E. Chamorro Greca and J.C. Agulla, *De la industria al poder* (Buenos Aires, Ediciones Líbera, 1966); Juan Carlos Agulla, "Poder, Comunidad y Desarrollo Industrial; la estructura del poder en una comunidad urbana en desarrollo: Córdoba", *Aportes*, 1966, 2, pp. 80-105.

2. Floyd Hunter, *Community Power Structures, A Study of Decision Makers,* (North Carolina: The University of North Carolina Press, 1953); D.C. Miller, "Industry and Community Power Structure: A Comparative Study of an American and an English City", *American Sociological Review*, 1958, February, 23, pp. 9-15; *Ibid.,* "Decision Making Cliques in Community Power Structure", *American Journal of Sociology*, 1958, November, 54, pp. 229-310.

3. In 1952 the IAME tractor factory was built and in 1955 and 1956 the FIAT motor, tractor, railway, and automobile factories and the KAISER automobile factory, respectively. It is worth noting that at the end of the 1920s the Military Aircraft Factory was built in Córdoba, which greatly influenced opening the way for the industrialization of Córdoba.

4. Juan Carlos Agulla, *op. cit.*, p. 81; *Ibid., Razón y sociedad,* (Tucumán: Universidad Nacional de Tucumán, 1965), p. 79 ff.

5. D.C. Miller, E. Chamorro and J.C. Agulla, *op. cit.*, p. 110 ff.

6. *Ibid.,* p. 93 ff.

7. *Ibid.,* p. 44 ff.

8. *Ibid.,* p. 45; J.C. Agulla, *Razón y sociedad, op. cit.*, pp. 105-27.

9. Cf. T.B. Bottomore, *Minorías selectas y sociedad* (Madrid: Biblioteca Universitaria Gredos, 1965), p. 7 ff; Vilfredo Pareto, *Trattato di Sociologia Generale* (Florence: G. Barbera Editore, 1916); *Ibid.,* "Forma y Equilibrio sociales" (Madrid: *Revista de Occidente,* 1966); Gaetano Mosca, *The Ruling Class: Elementi di Scienza Politica* (New York: McGraw-Hill Book Co., 1939); Max Weber, *Staatssoziologie* (Berlin: Duncker & Humbolt, 1956); Robert Michels, *Political Parties* (Glencoe: The Free Press, 1949); James Burnham, *The Machiavellians: Defenders of Freedom*

(London: Putnam & Co., 1943); Hans P. Dreitzel, *Elitebegriff und Sozialstruktur* (Stuttgart: Ferdinand Enke Verlag, 1922); C. Wright Mills, *La élite del poder* (Mexico: Fondo de Cultura Económica, 1957).

10. Cf. T.B. Bottomore, *op. cit.*, p. 7-28.

11. *Ibid.;* Cf. J.C. Agulla, *Razón y sociedad, op. cit.*, pp. 213-214.

12. D. C. Miller and others, *op. cit.*, pp. 142-43.

13. For this, consult the Bibliography of footnote 9.

14. These distinctions are not to be construed as having general application, but only refer to Córdoba.

15. Cf. Vilfredo Pareto, *op. cit.*, and Gaetano Mosca, *op. cit.*

16. Explanations of the development processes by symbols are very much debated in the theoretical field; nevertheless, we believe they continue to be useful. Cf. J.C. Agulla, *Razón y sociedad, op. cit.*, second part, p. 105 ff.; Gino Germani, *Politica y sociedad en una época de transición* (Buenos Aires: Paidós, 1962).

17. With this assertion one attempts to touch upon the iciest problem of theoretical discussion about the *élites;* and when Marx refers to organizing the proletariat to constitute a revolutionary force, that is, a factor or agent of change, besides other elements, he has in mind the *ruling élites* of this proletariat, who determine the mechanisms of social change and revolution. There is no contradiction, as some theorists have propounded, between *ruling élites* and proletariats.

18. A. Ferrer, *La economia argentina* (Mexico: Fondo de Cultura Económica, 1963); W. Rostow, *Las etapas del crecimiento económico* (Mexico: Fondo de Cultura Económica, 1961); Raúl Prebisch, *Hacia una dinámica del desarrollo latinoamericano* (Mexico: Fondo de Cultura Económica, 1963); Gino Germani, *op. cit.*

19. Gino Germani, *op. cit.;* J.C. Agulla, *Razón y sociedad, op. cit.*, p. 105.

Chapter II

1. Cf. Ernesto Garzón-Valdés, "Die Universitätsreform von Córdoba," *Grundzüge des lateinamerikanischen Hochschulwesens,* Hanns-Albert Steger (hrg.) (Baden Baden, Nomos Verlagsgesellschaft, 1965), pp. 163-218. There is an ample bibliography in this work.

2. The "Manifesto" rudely attacks the Cordobese aristocracy and criticizes it for its alliance with the Church and the Clergy. In the time of the University Reform, according to reports, days of great violence occurred during the confrontation between the students and the university authorities; even the public took part in these violent scenes.

3. Gabriel del Mazo, V.R. Haya de la Torre, Palcos, Julio V. González, J.C. Mariátegui, F.J. Vocos, etc. Cf: bibliography of Note 1.

4. D.C. Miller, E. Chamorro and J.C. Agulla, *op. cit.*, p. 94, figure 2.

5. *Ibid.*, p. 80, figure 1.

6. A. Capdevilla, *Córdoba del recuerdo* (Buenos Aires: Espasa-Calpe, 1939); Ramón J. Cárcano, *Mis primeros ochenta años* (Buenos Aires: Sudamericano, 1944); R. de Ferrari Rueda, *Córdoba histórica* (Córdoba: author's edition, 1943); Manuel López Cepeda, *Marcos Juárez. Su vida y su tiempo* (Córdoba: Universidad Nacional de Córdoba, 1962); Enrique Martínez Paz, *La formación histórica de Córdoba* (Córdoba: Universidad Nacional de Córdoba, 1941); Manuel Río and Luis Achával, *Geografía de la Provincia de Córdoba* (Buenos Aires: Edición Oficial, 1905); Alfredo Terzaga, *Geografía de Córdoba* (Córdoba: Assandri, 1963); etc.

7. Domingo F. Sarmiento, *Facundo* (Buenos Aires: Espasa-Calpe, 1951) p. 86 ff.

8. Perhaps as a synthesis of the description of the doctoral aristocracy of Córdoba, the following words of Manuel Río will serve, and which have been quoted so frequently in this volume: "...at the social crest were found men of letters, the clergy, and the haughty functionaries coming, directly or indirectly, from the metropolis. Of pure lineage, trustees of all the knowledge of the age, possessors of exalted and dignified offices, the Doctors, Licenciados, Masters, and Bachelors of the Casa de Trejo constituted a free and universally respected aristocracy, pompous and formalistic, cultivated and devout, imbued with the honor of their title and full of their well-known superiority over the common people. The aura with which the Colony was surrounded resisted the levelling commotions of the Independence. The marks of its influence are easily seen in the cloth of national life. And even today (1905) the doctoral parchment holds a certain prestigious lustre,

towards which the youth in the university halls hurl themselves." It is well to remember that this description was made in 1905 by an active participant in the history of Córdoba at that time.

9. The role fulfilled by a social stratum, in our case the doctoral aristocracy, in the power structure, must determine its internal structure; if there are changes in the functions of a stratum, especially in the functions of government, there will tend to be changes in its very structure; therefore, for example, an aristocracy must change insofar as do its functions in the power structure.

10. Cf. note 8.

11. Manuel Río, *op. cit.,* cf. note 8.

12. *Ibid.*

13. *Ibid.* It should be pointed out that all these statements have been checked with documents of the time, especially with newspapers and works on the political history of the City of Córdoba. We have found some biographies on Marcos Juárez, Ramón J. Cárcano, Miguel Juárez Celman, etc. most useful.

14. E. Martínez Paz, *op. cit.;* Manuel Río and Luis Achával, *op. cit.;* Alfredo Terzaga, *op. cit.,* p. 290.

15. J.C. Agulla, *Razón y sociedad, op. cit.,* Second Part.

16. Cf. note 14. These expressions were checked with documents and news chronicles, but above all in conversations with the informants of this investigation, some of whom had the opportunity to live with them during this period.

17. *Ibid.*

18. *Ibid.*

19. This restraint is noted, according to the informants of the investigation, in certain depreciative expressions used against the estancieros by the doctorales, especially in that which referred to the violation of the standards of courtesy and customs. The expression "guaso del campo" ["country rustic"] or "gaucho" alluded to this fact. The key informants eloquently pointed out these facts.

20. D.F. Sarmiento, *op. cit.,* p. 86 ff.

21. Manuel Río and L. Achával, *op. cit.;* A. Terzaga, *op. cit.,* p. 290.

22. *Ibid.* News chronicles mentioned this. The key informants concurred. Cf. Manuel López Cepeda, *Gente, casas y calles de Córdoba* (Córdoba: Biffignandi Ediciones, 1966); Emilio Sánchez,

140

Sirviendo a la democracia (Córdoba: Author's editions, 1957).

23. A. Terzaga, *op. cit.*, p. 290.

24. The National Censuses of 1895 and 1914 give the following figures:

$$1895: \quad 54,673$$
$$1914: \quad 134,935$$

25. A. Terzaga, *op. cit.*, p. 290 ff.

26. *Ibid.*

27. An approximate quantitative proportion exists between the highest social stratum and the rest of the population; apparently it does not exceed 3 or 4 percent of the population. In the case of Córdoba, there would be some 4000 persons belonging to some 100 families.

28. The following statistical table on the population of Córdoba will show the process of increase in population:

CN	1869	34,458	E.	1938	323,360
CM	1887	62,247	E.	1940	341,888
CP	1890	65,472	CN	1947	386,828
CN	1895	54,763	E.	1950	412,641
E.	1900	72,500	CN	1960	589,153
CP	1906	92,776	E.	1965	683,628
CN	1914	134,935	E.	1967	727,850
			E.	1970	799,617

(CN: National Census; CM: Municipal Census; CP: Provincial Census; E: estimation. The source of these figures is the Dirección General de Estadísticas, Censos e Investigaciones of the Province of Córdoba.)

29. Cf. E. Martínez Paz, *op. cit.*

30. Emiliano Endrek, *El mestizaje en el Tucumán* (Córdoba: Universidad Nacional de Córdoba, 1967); R. Miatello, *Población de la Provincia de Córdoba* (Córdoba: Printed by the Universidad Nacional de Córdoba, 1959); A. Terzaga, *op. cit.*, Chapters VII, VIII and IX.

31. *Ibid.* The key informants illustrated these racial prejudices with certain epithets such as "negro," "Chinese," "gaucho," etc.

32. E. Martínez Paz, *op. cit.*

Chapter III

1. J.C. Agulla, *Razón y sociedad, op. cit.*, Second Part; *Ibid., De la industria al poder, op. cit.*, First Part.

2. Cf. Bibliography of Note 2 of Chapter I.

3. D.C. Miller, E. Chamorro and J.C. Agulla, *De la industria al poder, op. cit.;* Juan Carlos Agulla, "Córdoba, Poder y Desarrollo," *loc. cit.*

4. Cf. Note 8 of Chapter II.

5. D.C. Miller, E. Chamorro and J.C. Agulla, *op. cit.*, p. 117 ff.

6. *Ibid.*, p. 117.

Chapter V

1. José Luis de Imaz, *La clase alta de Buenos Aires* (Buenos Aires: Colección Estructura, National University of Buenos Aires, 1962).

2. *Ibid.;* also, José Luis de Imaz, *Los que mandan* (Buenos Aires: Eudeba, 1964).

3. This phenomenon is seen in many studies made in Europe on the upper and traditional bourgeois. Germany, France, and England had an aristocracy which was created on the basis of the industrial tadition. The United States is the only one [here] which has formed one. In our country, the aristocracies of Tucumán and, to some extent, Mendoza have something similar.

4. The aristocracy of Córdoba has been, in general, fairly poor and has been getting progressively more poor. It only retains as "noble title" the "doctoral parchment" which it traditionally possesses, which justifies its position in the social stratification of the City. Certainly, it does not command any other similarity to European nobility, since family tradition or pure blood do not appear to be so decisive, owing to the mechanisms it has institutionalized for access to matrimony: the university diploma and pure moral and family life.

Appendix I

1. Cf. Delbert C. Miller, Eva Chamorro Greca, and Juan Carlos Agulla: *De la industria al poder,* Ediciones Libera. Buenos Aires, 1966; Cf. also Delbert C. Miller, Eva Chamorro Greca, and Juan Carlos Agulla: "The Power Structure of an Argentine City: A Comparative Study of International Design," *American Journal of*

Sociology, 1966; *ibid.,* "The Community Power Perspective and Community Role Definitions of North American Business Executives in an Argentine Community," *Administrative Science Quarterly,* Ithaca, N.Y., 1965; Cf. Floyd Hunter: *Community Power Structure* (A Study of Decision Makers), The University of North Carolina Press, 1953; Delbert C. Miller: "Industry and Community Power Structure: A Comparative Study of an American and an English City," *American Sociological Review,* 23 (February 1958), pp. 8-15; *ibid.,* "Decision-Making Cliques in Community Power Structure: A Comparative Study of an American and an English City," American Journal of Sociology, 54 (November 1958), pp. 229-310.

2. The cities studied were Córdoba, Seattle (Washington State), Bristol (England), and Atlanta (studied by Floyd Hunter). The common variables, in general, were an approximately equal population, a similar political, administrative and commercial center; a similar "western" type of culture; a university center, and, essentially, an industrial center. Cf. Delbert C. Miller, Eva Chamorro Greca, and Juan Carlos Agulla: *De la industria al poder, op. cit.*

3. However, two variables appeared as distinctive in Córdoba: the function discharged by the Catholic church in the life of the city for many years, and the role of the National University of Córdoba since 1613. These characteristics, doubless very important relating to decisions taken in the community, were not possessed by the other American and British cities. But two variables had a very different character in the Argentine city: the recency of the process of industrialization, and the social structure of Argentine society.

4. Cf. Juan Carlos Agulla: *Razón y Sociedad,* Cuadernos de Humanitas, National University of Tucumán, Tucumán, 1966; also, G. Germani: *Política y Sociedad an una época de transición,* Editorial Paidos, Buenos Aires, 1962.

5. *Ibid.;* also, Delbert C. Miller, Eva Chamorro Greca, and Juan Carlos Agulla: *De la industria al poder, op. cit.,* first part.

6. *Ibid.;* Cf. Eva Chamorro Greca: *La estructura de la familia en Córdoba* (in press); Juan Carlos Agulla: "Aspectos sociales del proceso de industrialización en una comunidad urbana," *Revista Mexicana de Sociología,* XXV, May-August 1963, Vol. XXV, No.

2, pp. 743-772; Eva Chamorro Greca, C.O. Ramírez, and E. Saforcada. "Actitud y cambio social," in *Sociología y las Sociedades en desarrollo industrial*, papers of the XX Congress of the International Institute of Sociology, Córdoba, Vol. V, pp. 117-124.

7. Cf. J. Medina Echavarría: *Aspectos sociales del Desarrollo Económico*, Editorial Andrés Bello, Santiago, Chile, 1959.

8. Cf. Juan Carlos Agulla: "Aspectos sociales del proceso de industrialización en una comunidad urbana," *op. cit.*

9. C. Wright Mills: *La élite del poder*, Fondo de Cultura Económica, third edition, Mexico, 1963.

10. *Ibid.;* also see: W. Zapf *et al, Beiträge zur Analyse der deutschen Oberschicht*, Studien und Berichte aus dem Sozialogischen Seminar der Universität Tübingen, 1964; H.D. Lasswell and A. Kaplan: *Power and Society*, Yale University Press, New Haven and London, 1950; Gaetano Mosca: *The Ruling Class*, translated by H. D. Kahn, McGraw-Hill Paperbacks, New York, Toronto, and London, 1939; J. L. de Imaz, *Los que mandan*, Informes de Eudeba, Editorial Universitaria de Buenos Aires, 1964; *ibid.: La clase alta de Buenos Aires*, Colección Estructura, National University of Buenos Aires, Buenos Aires, 1962.

11. Cf. note 1 and W. V. D'Antonio and W.H. Form: *Influentials in Two Border Cities* (A Study in Community Decision-Making), University of Notre Dame Press, 1965; *ibid.*, "Integration and Cleavage Among Influentials in Two Border Cities," *American Sociological Review*, 24 (December 1959), pp. 804-814; W.H. Form and D.C. Miller: *Industry, Labor and Community*, Harper and Brothers, New York, 1960.

12. *Ibid.;* also Cf. D.C. Miller, E. Chamorro Greca, and J.C. Agulla: *De la industria al poder, op. cit.*

13. *Ibid.*

14. Cf. note 1.

15. The methodology is all explained in D.C. Miller, E. Chamorro Greca, and J.C. Agulla: *De la industria al poder, op. cit.;* Cf. also in the works already published in *The American Journal of Sociology* and in *The Administrative Sciences Quarterly*.

16. Cf. C. Wright Mills: *op. cit.*

17. Cf. Figures 1 and 2, pp. 118 and 119.

18. Cf. *De la industria al poder, op. cit.*

19. Cf. D.C. Miller: "Industry and Community Power Structure. A Comparative Study of an American and an English City," *loc. cit.;* and Floyd Hunter: *op. cit.,* Cf. graph, Figures 1 and 2.

20. These data were obtained at the time of the investigation. It is useful to point out that at the moment of investigation the city of Córdoba was intervened by the National Government and elections were already in sight, since they were already called and political activity was fairly intense.

21. An investigation by Harvard University, directed by Professor Alex Inkeles, allowed one to perceive the extent of these data in Córdoba, notwithstanding a certain "resistance" in Córdoba to the application of a "pattern of investigation so abstract."

22. Cf. *De la industria al poder,* op. cit.; also, D.C. Miller, Eva Chamorro Greca, and J.C. Agulla: "The Community Power Perspectives and Community Role Definitions of North American Business Executives in an Argentine Community," *loc. cit.*

23. This problem was investigated, and the difference in degree of participation appearing between the top influentials of Córdoba and the top influentials of the American and British cities is quite considerable. This is seen in the following table:

Percentage of reciprocal relations and participation in voluntary associations by the top influentials of Seattle (in the United States), of Bristol (in England), and of Córdoba (in Argentina).

Cities	Percentage of reciprocal relations	Percentage of voluntary association
Seattle (United States)	106.8	11.6
Bristol (England)	107.1	10.5
Córdoba (Argentina)	77.1	3.0*

*Difference between the mean of an Argentine city (Córdoba) and the means of an American city (Seattle) and an English city (Bristol) with a level of significance of 0.01.

Index